1/90
14

School Yard-Bac Cycles of Science

CC
J372.3
DEB

by
Jerry DeBruin

illustrated by Elaine Scott

Cover by Jeff Van Kanegan

Copyright © Good Apple, Inc., 1989

ISBN No. 0-86653-489-X

Printing No. 987654321

Good Apple, Inc.
Box 299
Carthage, IL 62321-0299

10/89 $10 95

Special Thanks

The author thanks Mrs. Ruth Flaskamp, fifth grade teacher at Stranahan Elementary School, Sylvania, Ohio, for permission to field-test this book with youngsters.

The author thanks the following youngsters who field-tested this book on the school yard at school and in their backyards at home. Special thanks go to their parents who demonstrated patience and understanding and became partners in the learning process with their youngsters. The youngsters are Jenny Dibble, Jaimie Gerity, Corey Goldberg, Jamie Hartman, Brad Hesser, Michael Hurd, Karen Knemeyer, Kelly Lauger, Nicole Messenger, Sabrina McCue, Steve Miller, Ben Nachtrab, Daniel Posner, Molly Quinn, Elizabeth Reeping, Adam Saggese, Sara Slaughterbeck, Jean Tilley, Angela Williams and Paul Yuen.

The author thanks his university students who field-tested this book with youngsters. The author thanks the students for their suggestions, thoughtful ideas and comments.

The author thanks Mrs. Tina Hughes, secretary, who typed the original version of this book before it was sent to the publisher.

The author also thanks Mr. Thomas Gibbs, B.S. Ed., M.Ed., J.D., retired teacher, counselor, naval officer and locomotive engineer for his kind contributions, suggestions and assistance in making this book the best book that it could be.

Thank you ~

To: _____

From: _____

Dedication

To my brother, Eugene DeBruin, who taught me

THE CYCLE OF LIFE . . .

With a missing link.

The missing link in Eugene DeBruin's

LIFE CYCLE . . .

Will be forged by his eventual release;

Or, with information on his current fate and where-abouts

GIVEN TO THOSE WHO KEEP THE VIGIL . . .

By those who hold him in chains.

THA PA CHON VILLAGE,

KHAMMOUANE PROVINCE, LAOS

Left to right: American, Eugene Henry DeBruin; Thais, Pisidhi Indradat, Prasit Promsuwan, Prasit Thanee; Hong Kong Chinese, To Yick Chiu.

The Clock of Life

The clock of life is wound but once,
  And no person has the power,
To tell just when the clock, will stop,
  At late or early hour.
Now is the only time you own,
  Live, Love, Toil with a Will—
Place no faith in "tomorrow" for
  The clock may then be still.

author unknown

American Civilian Detainee in Asia

Eugene Henry DeBruin, 1960

Eugene, a U.S. civilian employed by an independent airline in Laos, was shot down near Tchepone, Laos, on September 5, 1963. He was on a supply mission which included dropping rice and buffalo meat to Lao villagers. He was first listed as missing.

After several weeks, the Pathet Lao told us that Eugene and four other crew members survived the crash. They took the picture shown at the left which clearly shows the five as confirmed prisoners of the Pathet Lao. In 1964, the five escaped but were recaptured. In 1966, the five, along with two other United States personnel, escaped. One American and one Thai reached safety after the seven had previously separated into four groups to avoid recapture.

A subsequent report notes that Eugene was being held as a prisoner in Southeast Savannakhet Province, Laos, in January, 1968.

In 1982 a high ranking Lao colonel, Khamla Koephithoune, supplied unconfirmed information about Eugene to a visiting U.S. delegation. Today, information continues to surface that indicates Eugene is still being held captive. Members of Eugene's family firmly believe that officials of the Lao People's Democratic Republic should release Eugene Henry DeBruin immediately or provide confirmed, well-documented evidence of his current fate and whereabouts.

GA1084

Table of Contents

GA1084

Summer follows winter,
new moon follows old,
day follows night.
. . . the universe is not static;
every component from an electron to a galaxy is continually
moving and such movement cannot proceed forever in the same
direction. Sooner or later it must complete a circle, or stop and
return in the opposite direction.

J.L. Cloudsley-Thompson

GA1084

INTRODUCTION: a Note to Teachers and Parents

Dear Friends,

Thank you for the many kind comments about my previous nineteen books—Touching and Teaching Metrics Series; *Cardboard Carpentry; Creative, Hands-On Science Experiences;* the Young Scientists Explore Series, Intermediate; *Scientists Around the World* and *Look to the Sky*—all published by Good Apple, Inc., from 1977 to 1988.

This book, *School Yard-Backyard Cycles of Science*, is written as a result of your comments and suggestions, comments that suggested a need for child-centered, hands-on activity sheets which could be duplicated for students' use. *School Yard-Backyard Cycles of Science* is an attempt to meet this need.

School Yard-Backyard Cycles of Science is written for people of all ages and for those in any occupation. Classroom teachers, administrators, youth leaders, camp guides and parents will find it useful. The book focuses on the use of *common, everyday materials* some of which can be obtained free or purchased rather inexpensively, or found around the home, school or in the community. Major emphasis is placed on *starter activities*, activities designed to prompt children to ask "Why" or "What would happen if" type questions about science events.

In an ever-changing society, there is a growing need for youngsters to become actively involved in problem-solving science with application of the knowledge gained in school directly to the home setting. *School Yard-Backyard Cycles of Science* meets this need with its unique contents and school/home format.

School Yard-Backyard Cycles of Science is grounded in and supports current research findings in science education. Convenient, ready-to-use teacher and student materials and activities support these findings in at least eight ways. First, the activities are "hands-on" and reinforce the notion that people learn science best by becoming involved in *concrete experiences,* rather than by mere rote memorization of abstract, trivial and unrelated facts. Second, concepts mastered by doing the activities in the book are appropriate for the *developmental level* of elementary, middle, and junior high school students. All youngsters, teachers, and parents who choose to become involved will find the activities challenging and useful. Third, the activities presented in the book help teachers, youngsters and parents reach the #1 goal of education which is to stimulate people to *think*, then take *action*. In addition, the activities feature an extensive utilization of *higher order thinking and process skills*. Memorization of irrelevant facts, at the knowledge level only, is kept to a minimum. Fourth, activities in the book help teachers and parents involve youngsters in experiences that will enable youngsters to master concepts well-beyond those found in the standard curriculum in commercially available textbook series. Fifth, the activities feature the *integration of science with other academic disciplines.* By participating in the activities, youngsters, teachers, and parents experience an interdisciplinary, integrated view of science with an emphasis on learning holistic cycles of science. Sixth, because of the unique school/home format of *School Yard-Backyard Cycles of Science*, the activities enable youngsters to apply knowledge gained in school directly to their home setting. Parental involvement is stressed by doing activities at home which emanate from, and are directly related to, key concepts taught in school. The transfer of knowledge from school to home is stressed. Teachers, parents, and youngsters grow as a result of increased communication between the home and school. Seventh, *School Yard-Backyard Cycles of Science* is *child centered.* To accomplish this goal, a clear delineation of student rights is presented in the text along with appropriate child-centered activities. Lastly, *School Yard-Backyard Cycles of Science* provides necessary background information in the form of teacher tips and specific content information. Thus, it is hoped that teachers, youngsters, and parents will benefit by the renewed emphasis on content and methodology found in Parts One, Two and Three, and in an annotated Glossary itself.

My hope is that the information and activities in *School Yard-Backyard Cycles of Science* will touch many minds, hearts and hands and that much personal growth will be experienced by all who use the book. Keep in touch. Let me know how you are doing. It is always good to hear from you. Until then, best wishes for your continued growth as a scientist and as a complete human being.

Sincerely,

Jerry DeBruin

Jerry DeBruin

The Symbols of Cycles

DIRECTIONS: Read the names of the symbols in the outer ring. Starting at number 1, turn the page counterclockwise. In the blank by each cycle, write the number of the matching cycle. The first one is done for you.

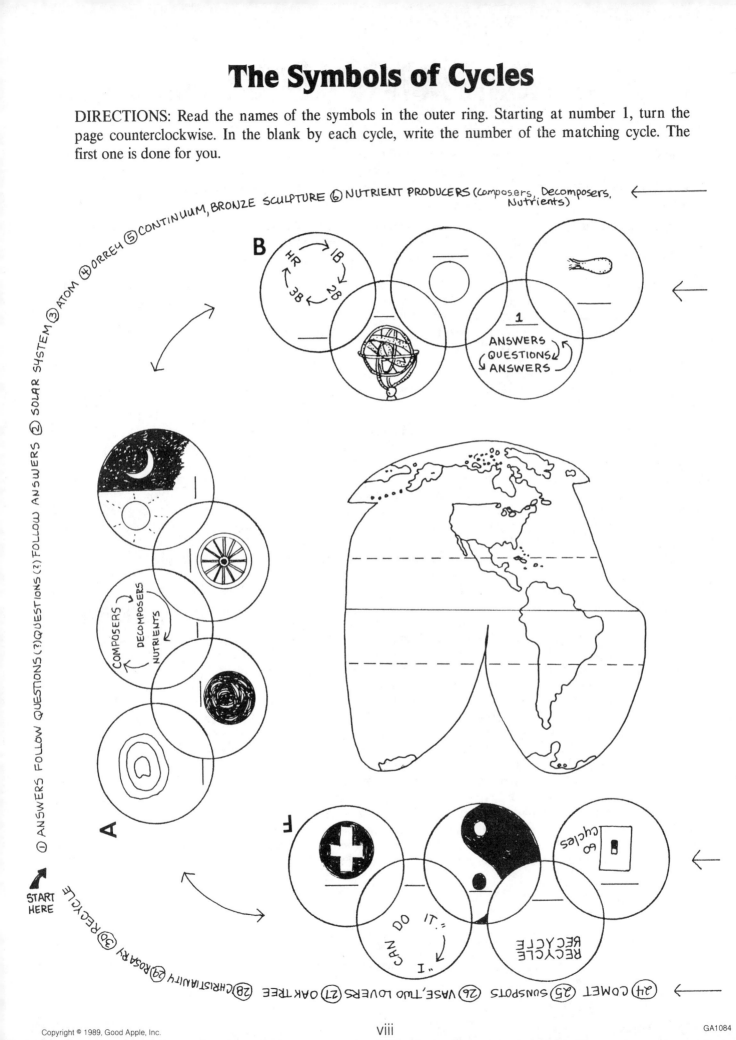

GA1084

The Symbols of Cycles

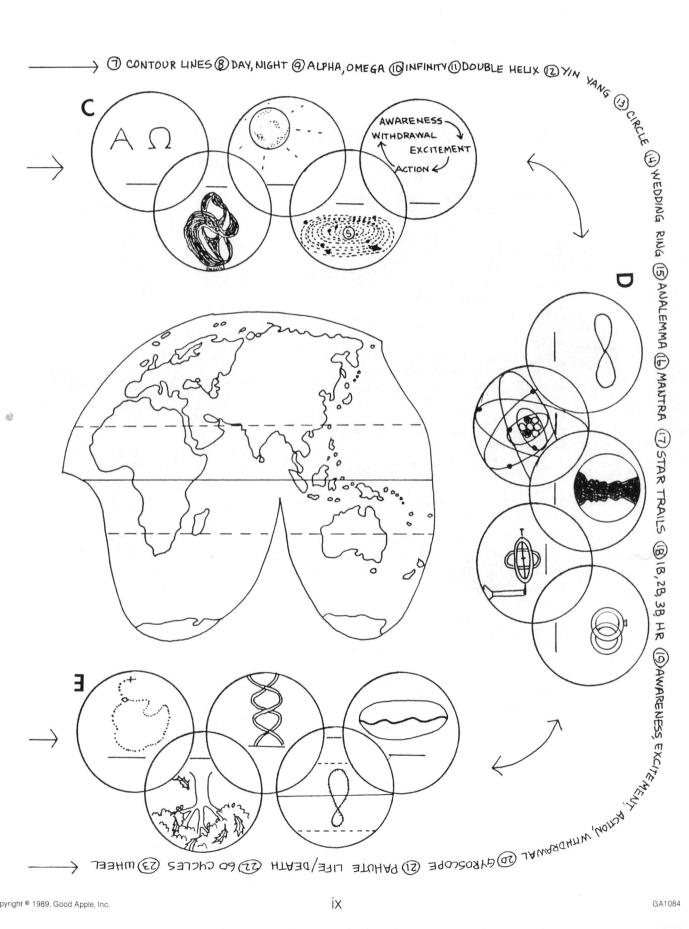

⑦ CONTOUR LINES ⑧ DAY, NIGHT ⑨ ALPHA, OMEGA ⑩ INFINITY ⑪ DOUBLE HELIX ⑫ YIN YANG ⑬ CIRCLE ⑭ WEDDING RING ⑮ ANALEMMA ⑯ MANTRA ⑰ STAR TRAILS ⑱ 1B, 2B, 3B, HR ⑲ AWARENESS, EXCITEMENT, ACTION, WITHDRAWAL ⑳ GYROSCOPE ㉑ PAIUTE LIFE/DEATH ㉒ 60 CYCLES ㉓ WHEEL

C

AWARENESS
WITHDRAWAL
EXCITEMENT
ACTION

D

E

GA1084

The following statement of students' rights lies at the heart of this book. Its primary purpose is to inspire teachers and parents to recognize student rights, maximize student learning and help students become contributing members to a democratic society.

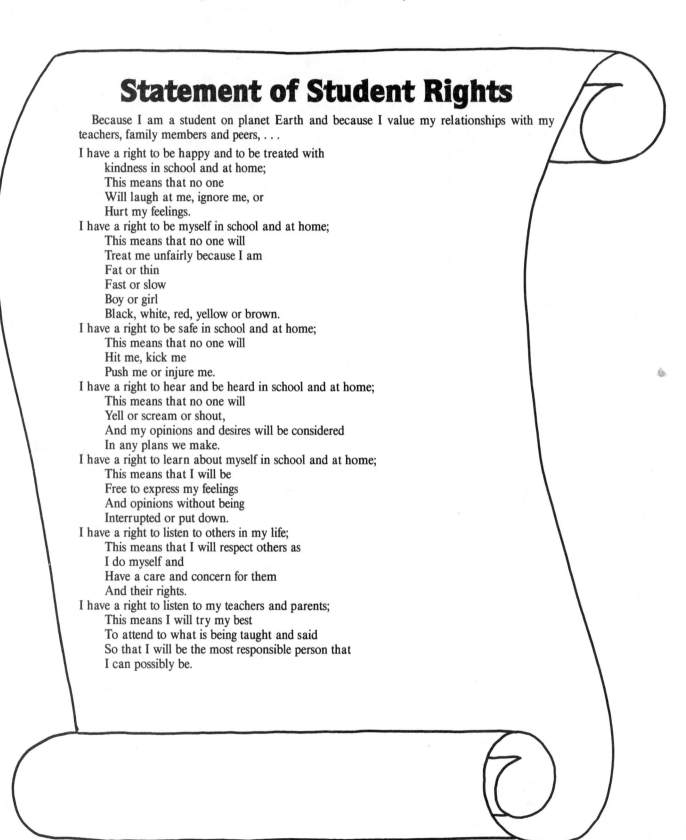

Statement of Student Rights

Because I am a student on planet Earth and because I value my relationships with my teachers, family members and peers, . . .

I have a right to be happy and to be treated with
    kindness in school and at home;
    This means that no one
    Will laugh at me, ignore me, or
    Hurt my feelings.

I have a right to be myself in school and at home;
    This means that no one will
    Treat me unfairly because I am
    Fat or thin
    Fast or slow
    Boy or girl
    Black, white, red, yellow or brown.

I have a right to be safe in school and at home;
    This means that no one will
    Hit me, kick me
    Push me or injure me.

I have a right to hear and be heard in school and at home;
    This means that no one will
    Yell or scream or shout,
    And my opinions and desires will be considered
    In any plans we make.

I have a right to learn about myself in school and at home;
    This means that I will be
    Free to express my feelings
    And opinions without being
    Interrupted or put down.

I have a right to listen to others in my life;
    This means that I will respect others as
    I do myself and
    Have a care and concern for them
    And their rights.

I have a right to listen to my teachers and parents;
    This means I will try my best
    To attend to what is being taught and said
    So that I will be the most responsible person that
    I can possibly be.

GA1084

Part One
Why Study School Yard-Backyard Cycles of Science?

Here are some pictures of teaching tips that you will encounter in this section.

GA1084

Basic Beliefs About How Youngsters Best Learn Science

*That youngsters best learn science when they are active learners engaged in "hands-on" activities rather than passive learners involved in activities that require mere rote memorization. In other words, youngsters learn by doing and then thinking about what they have done.

*That youngsters best learn science when they use the scientific method which features the use of the processes of science to promote meaningful learning. Some of these processes include imagining, creating, observing, classifying, measuring, predicting, experimenting, inferring, collecting, organizing and interpreting data, evaluating and communicating.

*That youngsters best learn science when they are engaged in "hands-on" activities that teach sequential science concepts appropriate for their developmental age level of maturity. Many "hands-on" activities require reading and writing skills that enable youngsters to master sequential science concepts.

*That youngsters best learn science when they develop an understanding of the *interdisciplinary nature of science* and recognize how science is an integral part of all other academic disciplines both in and outside of school.

*That youngsters best learn science when they attack problems that are directly related to their everyday lives. This allows youngsters to critically examine the sociological implications of technology-based decision making. In essence, youngsters need to know how to access and retrieve information in an effort to be the best youngsters they can be.

*That youngsters best learn science when they are engaged in scientific activities that provide experiences and information on *career opportunities* in science.

School Yard-Backyard Cycles of Science features a basic code of beliefs and values about how youngsters best learn science. Its pages are open for all to read and ponder.

QUESTIONS
ANSWERS

GA1084

Basic Beliefs About the Needs of Youngsters

Needs of youngsters are based upon a belief about how youngsters best learn science. These needs include the following:

*Youngsters have a need to experience science directly and participate in "hands-on" science activities. They need to understand that science is a human endeavor which does not have all the answers but does provide a method for asking questions.

*Youngsters have a need to know that science is an integral part of life. They need to first develop and then master the process skills inherent in the scientific method in an effort to identify and interpret interactions between both living and nonliving worlds and thus find their place in the overall cycle of life. The scientific method used in problem solving is unique to science and has valuable carryover to life in general.

*Youngsters have a need to develop and master reading and writing skills in science. These skills help youngsters master a sequence of science concepts appropriate for their developmental level of maturity. An understanding of these concepts helps youngsters to develop their own innate abilities to the fullest extent possible.

*Youngsters have a need to view the world with a holistic perspective. Science is viewed as being *interdisciplinary* and cyclic in nature with a vast potential for being an interest generator and motivator. By nature, science is *interdisciplinary* and can be used to stimulate student interest in other areas of the curriculum and life in general.

*Youngsters have a need to be provided with the opportunity to critically examine the possible sociological implications of technological decision making. As citizens in a democratic society, youngsters have the responsibility to make informed decisions about present and future scientific fields of study and understand what effects such studies have on a global society.

*Beyond preparation for citizenship, youngsters have a need for higher level experiences that demonstrate the value of science as a viable career choice. Many vocations in existence today will cease to exist tomorrow. The number of vocations that require a "hands-on," problem solving, challenging, holistic, creative interdisciplinary and ever-changing cyclic view of the world will show a marked increase in the future. Teachers and parents who involve youngsters in scientific activities provide opportunities for youngsters to identify science as a viable career choice.

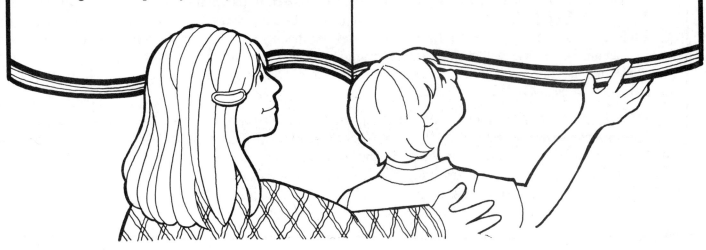

GA1084

The Cycle of Teaching

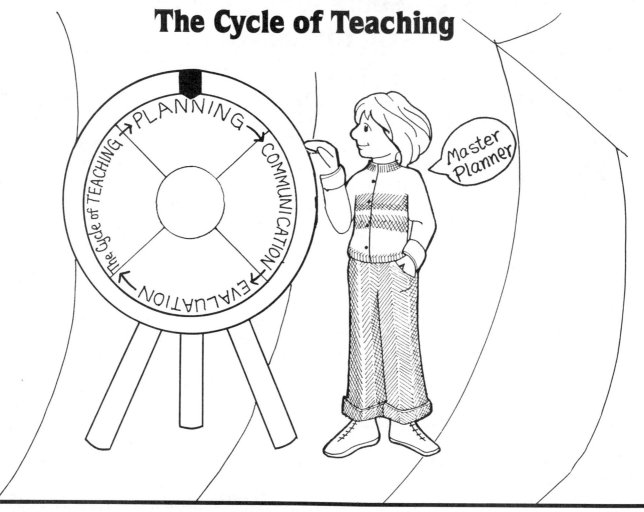

Planning the Interdisciplinary

Having a firm belief in, and understanding of, the rights and needs of youngsters and how they best learn science, teachers and parents can then plan appropriate learning experiences for youngsters. Many teachers and parents have found that the process of planning learning experiences for youngsters is similar to a spider spinning a web. This way of thinking helps you with both everyday and long-range planning. A web starts with any activity, idea, topic, or object that gets youngsters excited about learning. You or your youngsters merely choose a topic from something in which you and your youngsters are interested. Write the name of the topic in the center of a large piece of paper and circle it. Then mark the paper with the name of each academic discipline around the circle (see page 6). These disciplines are like an extension or spoke off the central topic. You and your youngsters can then think of learning activities that are related to the original idea in that discipline. Then write these topics down next to the original idea by connecting them with arrows or lines. Each idea you attach to the central idea becomes another idea and the cycle continues over and over again. Some ideas will overlap. Hence, from one idea flows many others in an interdisciplinary, cyclic manner. A web is never complete. You and your youngsters can always add at least one more idea to the cycle.

Once you have a fairly extensive web, you and your youngsters can hang the web up for all to use. Anyone can suggest ideas. You may also want to keep a copy on file so you can suggest future activities to the youngsters. Used in this way, the web becomes a master plan which can be used as a guide to extend learning. You and your youngsters need only to remember that all the ideas do not have to be studied, and if an idea or activity develops that was not on the original plan, that is okay, too.

GA1084

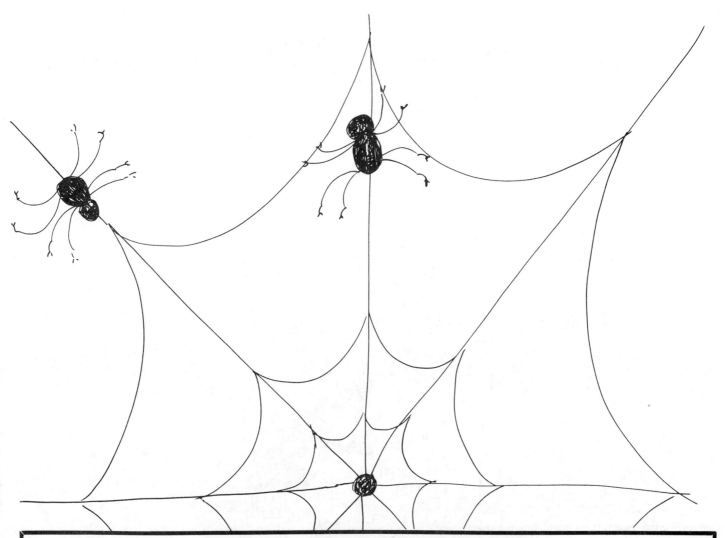

Science Web Experience

One advantage of a web experience is that teachers, parents and youngsters can plan activities in advance. In the example on page 6, teachers, parents and youngsters obtain reference books and manipulative materials for studying the web of science. Resource people such as various speakers can be contacted for assistance. By doing this you help get the study off the ground. A special bonus includes the meeting of a wide variety of people from a number of disciplines and occupations who are willing to share their experiences with your youngsters.

You may want to extend the use of your web by making a record of the actual ideas in which the youngsters become involved during the study and then compare it to the original web. This helps you write future webs that are more in tune with your youngsters' interests and needs. Keep a copy of all your webs for future use. A sample web is found on page 6. Included are page numbers of suggested activities found in this book. I'm still spinning the second web. You too will be able to spin many more by using you and your youngsters' vivid imaginations and spinning power. By the way, did you know that there are individuals who make their living by helping spiders spin webs? Yes, they tickle real spiders' bellies so the spiders spin more webs which are eventually used as crosshairs in scopes for rifles, telescopes and other instruments. That's true. Recently, a spider fixed a telescope that was ruined by an errant fly. The fly fell into the telescope and broke the strands of spider web that serve as the instrument's crosshairs. Knowing that human hair is too thick for the crosshairs in a telescope, a spider was called upon to spin a web. After being quieted down in a box to prevent the spider from spinning little blobs of thread, the calm spider spun a uniform thread that was used to repair the telescope. Thus, this microscopic gift of a spider web is now being used to explore the vast heavens.

GA1084

A Sample Interdisciplinary Science Web Experience

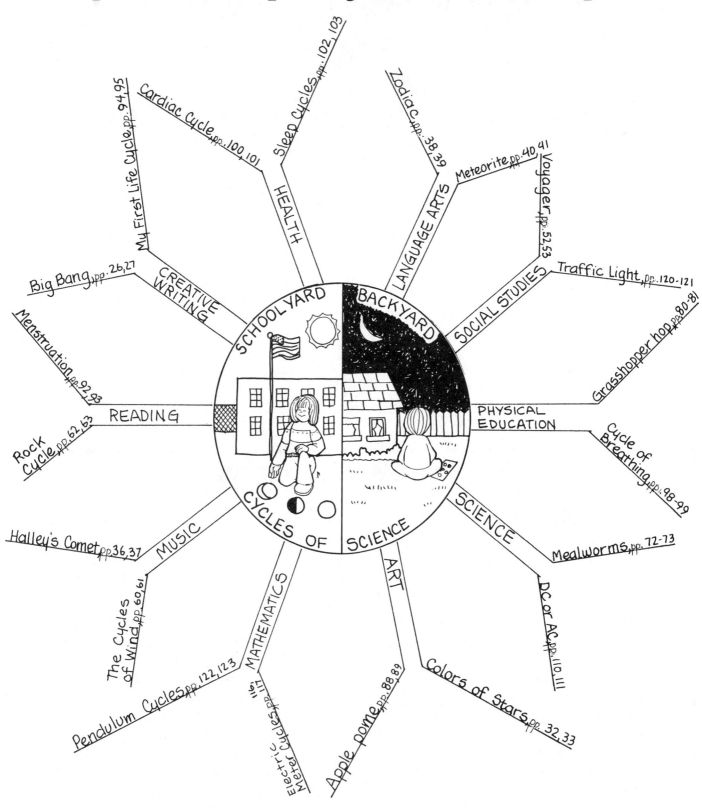

School Yard-Backyard Cycles of Science features interdisciplinary hands-on activities. This interdisciplinary web features ten academic disciplines and twenty related activities found in this book. It is hoped that you and your youngsters will add to this web or spin many more webs on your own.

6

GA1084

Communicating the Interdisciplinary Science Web Experience

After you have planned an interdisciplinary science web experience, you may use some of the following strategies to promote communication between you and your youngsters. Some of these strategies include the following:

Computer-Assisted Instruction
*Contracts
Demonstrations
Group Discussion with Debate (Valuing)
Independent Studies
Individualized Instruction
Large Group Convergent Inquiry
Large Group Divergent Inquiry
Learning Activity Packages (Lap)

*Learning Centers
Lecture Expository Instruction
One on One Techniques
Peer Mentor Techniques
Peer Tutoring Techniques
Programmed Instruction
Simulations and Games
Small Group Techniques

*In an attempt to meet the needs of *each* youngster, some teachers and parents use learning centers and contracts. These are highlighted in *School Yard-Backyard Cycles of Science.*

7

GA1084

Using Learning Centers to Enhance School/Home Communication

WHAT ARE LEARNING CENTERS?

Learning centers are used by teachers, parents and youngsters as a method to enhance communication between various individuals and the world around them. As teachers and parents we know that youngsters are unique human beings. We know that youngsters learn at different rates, have different styles, need a variety of experiences to learn and some need more experiences than others. Most importantly, we know, from experience, that youngsters are most interested in their learning and learn most effectively when they are actively involved in their learning. One way to get youngsters actively involved is by using manipulative materials in learning centers. As teachers and parents, it is important for us to put into action the following Chinese proverb by using manipulative materials:

I Hear and I Forget
I See and I Remember
I Do and I Understand

CHINESE PROVERB

In school or at home, learning centers are specific places in space that contain activities which help youngsters get in touch with their world by understanding specific science concepts. They supply welcome and wholesome alternatives to seatwork at school. They emphasize an active, self-selecting and problem-solving approach to learning which is carried out by individuals and small groups of youngsters. In school, learning centers free the teacher from large group instruction and allow time for the teacher to work with individual youngsters in a more personalized manner. The same is true at home. In summary, learning centers can be used both in school and at home to enhance communication by:

*helping youngsters develop independent and self-directed learning skills
*introducing new concepts and skills for youngsters to learn
*reinforcing skills and concepts previously taught by teachers and parents
*providing enrichment experiences for *all* youngsters
*helping youngsters develop self-motivation and self-discipline through tools of self-assessment and personal satisfaction
*individualizing instruction so more attention can be given to specific youngsters, to those who need that extra help in the form of remedial activity and for those gifted youngsters who need those extra enrichment activities for further development of the self.
*developing reflective thinking abilities, skills, and personal introspection.

GA1084

Tips for Implementing Learning Centers

☞ Write the goals that you'd like to teach on a sheet of paper.
Example: I would like my youngsters to learn about the life cycle of a butterfly.

☞ Decide on a sequence of concepts that you'd like to teach, usually having simple to complex levels of difficulty.
Example of a simple concept: Life Cycle of a Butterfly
Example of a complex concept: Pheromone

☞ Decide on a sequence of activities that will help teach the sequence of concepts in the centers.
Example of a sequence of activities that teach a sequence of concepts:

Major Concept:	Life Cycle of a Butterfly	Activity: Place four cards (labeled Egg,
Subconcepts:	1. Egg	Larva [caterpillar], Pupa [chrysalis]
	2. Larva (caterpillar)	Adult) in correct order to show life
	3. Pupa (chrysalis)	cycle of a butterlfy.
	4. Adult	

☞ Communicate your goals and concepts to the youngsters by using activity cards, charts and tapes. These act as springboards into learning activities in your centers. Make at least one activity card per concept that you would like to teach. Write the name of the concept on the back of the activity card and laminate for durability. Your cards may look like this.

Example Card 1

Place the four cards in order to show how a butterfly grows. Use the answer key to check your answers. Draw and color the butterfly and each of its stages.

Reverse Side

Activity Card #1

Concept: Life Cycle of a Butterfly

Subconcepts: Egg, Larva (caterpillar), Pupa (chrysalis), Adult

GA1084

☞ Construct a student self-assessment form and teacher record keeping system for each center. These record keeping systems can be made by developing a list of the concepts in the order in which they are taught.

Example:

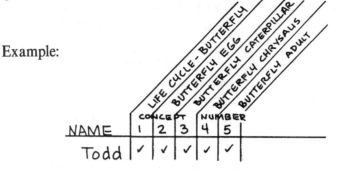

☞ Gather all manipulative materials needed for the centers.

Example: Cards labeled "egg," "larva (caterpillar)," "pupa (chrysalis)," "adult"; hand lens; clay; answer key.

☞ Identify designated spaces for the location of your centers and begin building them. Put newspapers on desks for messy experiments. Your room may look like this if you are teaching the concept of the life cycle of a butterfly.

GA1084

☞ Plan to manage the centers effectively. You may want to color code each learning center by using a different color of Con-Tact paper on large sheets of cardboard (see diagram on page 10). Color code coffee cans, one per center, with the same color of Con-Tact paper used on the cardboard in the center. Place matching color-coded sticks in the cans. (Popsicle sticks or tongue depressors work well for this.) Put only the number of sticks that are equivalent in number to the number of manipulatives you have in the center for each can. This will permit each youngster to work in the center effectively and prevents overcrowding. Place cans on a nearby table or desk. Youngsters choose appropriate center by selecting a matching color-coded stick for that center. If there are no sticks left in the can, this means that the center is full and no more youngsters can work in the center.

☞ Discuss with youngsters proper behavior for work in the center. On a chart, write down the procedures to be followed by all who work in the centers. Remind youngsters of these procedures often.

☞ Do a trial run. Actually teach youngsters how to use the centers. With help from youngsters, write down procedures for the centers. Include safety precautions. Remember that youngsters need time to learn how to use the centers.

☞ Start slowly. You may want to do a large group lesson first to get the science web experience underway, then gradually introduce the centers as youngsters become more familiar with the topic.

☞ Have youngsters record their observations and findings in their school yard-backyard science log books. See page 24 for sample page.

☞ Give youngsters immediate feedback on their performances by using Communication Cards, Progress Notes, or by having them use self-checking devices such as answer keys.

☞ Have youngsters build their own activities and learning centers to share with others. Some truly great discoveries have been made when using this technique.

☞ Have youngsters check their own progress by using a self-report form which includes a list of concepts to be mastered by the youngster.

☞ Communicate results of learning center activity to parents with the use of a sample Record Keeping System for Students and Parents which contains a list of concepts mastered by the youngster. Staple this to weekly or monthly newsletters that go home for parents to read.

☞ Share ideas with others including the principal, other teachers, special area personnel, parents, members of the custodial staff, media and community members. Sharing does help.

☞ Continue to grow in knowledge and understanding of yourself and others. The cycle of continually giving of yourself will lead to receiving many rewards in return. Remember the cycle of life:

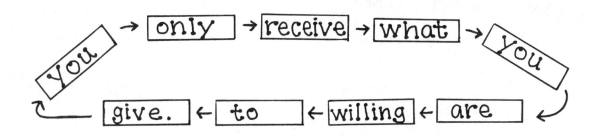

11

GA1084

Using Contracts to Enhance School/Home Communication

Another way to explore the world of school yard-backyard science is with the use of *contracts*. The contract system used in this book features "hands-on" science activities that are expanded upon by youngsters when involved in science. The advantages of using contracts are many. Some of these advantages include:

1. Youngsters learn independently and build upon innate potential abilities.
2. Youngsters work at their own rate.
3. Youngsters begin to assume responsibility for their own learning.
4. Youngsters develop interest and pride in their accomplishments.
5. Youngsters' frustrations and anxieties are reduced.
6. Youngsters choose among many diversified activities.
7. Youngsters choose their own individual learning styles.
8. Youngsters' family members are involved in the learning process.
9. Youngsters assess their own performance.
10. Youngsters share what they have learned with peers and family members.

Make multiple copies of the Master Independent Study Contract found on page 13. Distribute one contract per activity per student. To evaluate, check (√) the appropriate star at the bottom of the contract. Encourage youngsters and parents to assess the quality of performance by respectively coloring in or making a (+) on the appropriate star. Here's hoping you have many signed, completed and fulfilled contracts in your study of school yard-backyard science.

GA1084

Master Independent Study Contract

I _____ agree to complete the activity entitled
(name)

_____ found on page(s) _____
(title of activity)

in the book called *School Yard-Backyard Cycles of Science.*

I agree to begin my activity on _____ and have it completed and ready
(date)

to share with members of the class and my family on _____
(date)

I agree to use the scientific processes of inquiry and discovery and will turn to the following sources for information and assistance.

1. _____

2. _____

3. _____

4. _____

5. _____

Student Signature _____ Date _____

Parent Signature _____ Date _____

Teacher Signature _____ Date _____

. . . .

Date Begun _____

Date Completed _____

Date Shared with Class and Family _____

Official Seal of Approval: student (color in), parent (+ mark), teacher (✔ mark)

| Excellent | Good | Satisfactory | Needs Improvement | Repeat Activity |

GA1084

Special Tips for Parents Who Involve Youngsters in Backyard Cycles of Science

Dear Parents,

Parental guidance is the most important factor in helping youngsters become responsible citizens in a democratic society. The following tips are offered to encourage you to become partners with your youngster(s) in learning school yard-backyard science. Feel free to make copies of this and share with others.

1. **Be Positive.** When a person displays a positive feeling towards something, it encourages in others a similarly positive feeling towards that something. If you have a positive attitude toward backyard science, your children will develop that same positive attitude. Try to be positive about your children's work. Praise them when they succeed. Be there to help them when they are having problems. They need your support and encouragement. Feeling, touching, and responding to your children in a positive manner really does help.

2. **Be Aware of the Boy-Girl Syndrome.** Science is for boys and English is for girls. Right? No! Wrong. Stocking an aquarium and hatching chick eggs are important activities for both boys and girls. Try to eliminate sex-role stereotypes. Perhaps Mom could take the youngsters to a quarry to dig fossils while Dad whips up a salad for a nutritious meal. This practice helps promote the idea early in your children's lives that backyard science can be cooperatively done and thoroughly enjoyed by *all* members of the family.

3. **Be Aware of the Perfect Parent Syndrome.** Human beings are not perfect; we all make mistakes. Allow your children to make original mistakes, and then help them capitalize on these mistakes and learn from them. Jean Piaget once said that children learn more from their mistakes and wrong answers than they do from correct ones. The same holds true for adults. Permit your children to make original mistakes, but be sure they profit from them.

4. **Be Honest with Your Children.** Your children will ask many questions to which you may not know the answers. Be open and genuine in your responses. *Say* that you don't know the answer if you really don't know, but offer to help locate a source of information for possible answers and then follow through. Recently after an exciting science lesson, a pint-sized second-grade girl tugged on my pants leg and asked, "Do bears go to the bathroom when they hibernate?" I assured her that I really didn't know for sure but offered to pursue the question further with her. Together, we called the zookeeper, who provided us with limited information but encouraged us to continue our investigation. We dug deeper and found an animal physiology book that supplied more detailed information. The search for information continued with interesting ideas being discovered. The net result: we learned together from our experience—and a great deal at that. By the way, *do* bears really go to the bathroom when they hibernate? Yes, but only in small amounts because of low metabolic rate during hibernation, according to our expert. Others say that bears do *not* hibernate at all because their body temperature does not drop as the body temperature of true hibernating animals does. Our study continues today.

5. **Look Around You.** Coming up with ideas for the study of backyard science can be difficult, but it won't be if you look around you. Do you grow plants in your home or garden? Do you have small animals? Do you travel to recreational areas, the zoo, or the beach? If so, these areas are excellent starting points for launching the study of backyard science. Observe and discuss with your children what is happening around them in their immediate surroundings. Take your children to parks, science centers, farms, zoos, art museums, airports, factories, quarries, and pet shops to obtain further ideas for the study of backyard science.

6. **Seek Out People to Help You.** Contact people who have expertise in science and upon whom you can call to help with ideas on how to get started. Does your child have a favorite teacher in school or a relative who may help? High school science teachers and university science professors have ideas and may be willing to lend a hand. Local businesses and industries often have educational services divisions that are excellent sources for ideas. Keep a record of backyard science ideas and materials that you obtain from each source along with the names of key personnel and their telephone numbers for handy reference. Then contact these people for help.

7. **Get Books for Your Children.** Join and use the free public library. Take your children to the library and help them obtain library cards. Select and check out books on how to do backyard science projects. These books are excellent resources for starter ideas and do provide pertinent information that can be used. Books are fine because they often tell you how to get involved in backyard science. However, books will carry you and your child only so far. Actual materials that your children can feel, touch, and work with are much better when actually studying backyard science.

8. **Collect and Save Materials.** Collect materials from all sources. Think before you throw anything away. Could it be used to study backyard science? Guide your children in gathering materials, and develop ways to use and care for these materials. Such items as egg cartons, scrap pieces of lumber, and boxes are handy materials to collect for the study of backyard science.

14

9. **Work with Materials.** The single most important idea to remember is that your children must be free to work with actual materials. Inexpensive everyday household materials often work the best. Your children may enjoy mixing powders, growing plants, breeding fish, or building out of scrap cardboard a maze for a pet gerbil. Encourage your children to "mess about" with these ideas and materials instead of merely reading about scientific discoveries in a book. Put the following ancient Chinese proverb into action:

> I Hear and I Forget
> I See and I Remember
> I Do and I Understand

10. **Allow Time for Thinking and Exploring Alone.** You will want to provide ample time for your children to be alone. During this time your children will explore, ask questions, and think about what is being done. It is important to be patient with your children during this period of incubation. Keep the atmosphere relaxed. Be a good listener and learn right along with your children. Praise your children and help out, but be ever so careful not to do for them many things that they can do for themselves. Remember, it's your child's study, not necessarily yours.

11. **Stress "How-To" Skills.** You will want your children to develop some very special skills, called "process" skills, while studying backyard science. These skills should be stressed before the mastery of specific science facts. Some of these skills include observing, classifying, comparing, sorting, describing, inferring, and using space-time relationships. Your children will learn a great deal from observing an aquarium or an anthill, classifying animals by color and size, describing an experiment, making guesses about what might happen when solutions are added to various powders, and sketching the moon for a month. Encourage your children to use and extend all possible senses when learning the processes of science. Facts, too, are important, but the processes that your children use when arriving at science facts are more helpful because your children can use them to solve problems that come up in everyday life. A sense of accomplishment is gained and a positive self-concept is developed in your children.

12. **Examine Moral-Related Issues.** It is healthy to help your youngsters examine moral and value-related issues that may arise while doing backyard science. Your youngsters may ask why scientists sometimes sacrifice animals for experimentation purposes or why water becomes polluted. Gather information about these topics. Then help your youngsters explore the reasons experiments are conducted by scientists in various sit-uations in an effort to improve the lives of people on Earth.

13. **Daily Log of Backyard Science Activity.** You and your youngsters will want to keep accurate records of backyard science activity because many activities lead to school science fair projects. Information should be collected and recorded at regular intervals. You may want to help your youngsters keep a record of personal feelings about their study which then can be used in writing a paper for a local science fair, presentation, symposium, or developing a classroom project.

14. **Paper.** You will want to encourage your youngsters to use the daily log when writing a paper for a science fair project. The written paper should include a description of the problem studied, some guesses on how to solve the problem, the methods used for collecting information, testing procedures, and some tentative findings or conclusions. After the paper is written, help your youngsters plan and develop an attractive display for the home or school. Then go over some possible questions that visitors may ask your youngsters when they display their projects if they are entered in a science fair.

15. **The Fair.** It is vitally important that you and your youngsters go to the science fair together. Help your youngsters set up the display. Take photographs of their work and other entrants' displays. Save these ideas for future science projects. Have your youngsters develop a scrapbook of ideas. Encourage them to chat with others about their projects. Ideas breed ideas. We learn from each other.

16. **Follow-Up.** After awhile, your youngsters will reach a plateau in learning backyard science. Urge your youngsters to continue further research on the current project, dig a bit deeper, or explore other projects. Talk about the possibilities. Share. Evaluate past projects and plan future ones. Stress the importance of scientific research done for the betterment of humankind.

By following these tips, it is hoped that you as parents will become partners in the learning process with your youngsters. In addition to science, these tips are appropriate for the promotion of many other types of learning. Strive to be happy.

Your Friend,

Jerry DeBruin

GA1084

Evaluating the Interdisciplinary Science Web Experience

There are many different paths that teachers and parents can follow to evaluate their youngsters' learning. Some people use *cognitive* oriented evaluation tools like oral and/or written tests that feature fill-in-the-blank, matching and true-false questions. An example of this is found on page 17. Others focus on *psychomotor* skills such as having students actually build a model of a backyard pond or geological feature. (See page 18.) Still others focus on *affective* measures like trying to find out how students feel about themselves, about their work, about others and the world around them. (See page 19.) All three methods of evaluation, cognitive, psychomotor and affective, should be used in an effort to help individuals grow in understanding of the world about them and feelings toward themselves and others. In the latter case, smiley faces, personal letters, notes, interviews, individual conferences, student questionnaires and checklists can be used. Both you and your youngsters are encouraged to do many school yard-backyard science activities. You and the youngsters can write daily self-evaluations of your progress in science logs or diaries. (See page 24.) Fill out the instrument on page 19 before, in the middle of, and after the completion of a web experience to learn if you and your youngsters' attitudes have increased, decreased or remained the same. Point values can be assigned to each question, and you can record the attitude scores, calculate changes in attitudes over a period of time and note changes in such attitudes. A positive attitude ultimately leads to more positive attitudes. The cycle of being positive continues. It never ends but continues to grow and grow! *Remember* the following:

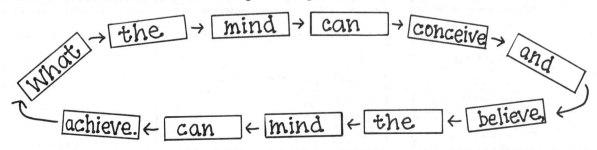

16

GA1084

Sample Cognitive Evaluation

These questions, based on Bloom's Taxonomy, are related to various pages in this book. The page number of the activity is listed in the upper left corner, the Taxonomy level in the upper right corner. Circle the letter of the response that best answers each question. Correct answers are found on page 141.

KNOWLEDGE: To know specific facts, ideas and vocabulary

p. 112   K
What does *D.C.* mean?
A. different current
B. dry cell
C. direct current
D. downward circuit

p. 87   K
The dome-shaped muscle that helps with breathing is the:
A. lung
B. bronchi
C. trachea
D. diaphragm

p. 89   K
The radial pulse is found at the:
A. neck
B. hand
C. arm
D. wrist

COMPREHENSION: To grasp concepts learned

p. 110   C
Which term means the simplest form of specific type of matter?
A. atom
B. molecule
C. element
D. nucleus

p. 63   C
Antennae of insects can be used for:
A. feeling, seeing, or hearing
B. placing eggs, feeling, or seeing
C. feeling, hearing, or smelling
D. seeing, hearing, or smelling

p. 47   C
Whether on Earth, on the moon, or in zero-gravity, what remains the same?
A. volume
B. density
C. temperature
D. mass

APPLICATION: To use information in a new situation

p. 94   AP
The correct measurement for your thumb is about:
A. 1 centimeter
B. 3 centimeters
C. 6 centimeters
D. 10 millimeters

p. 116   AP
In a series circuit, if one appliance doesn't work, what will happen to the others?
A. They'll all stay on.
B. They'll all go off.
C. The one next to it will go off.
D. About half will stay on.

p. 84   AP
In the food chain algae ⟶ limpets ⟶ starfish, what will happen if the number of limpets decreased?
A. starfish would decrease
B. algae would increase
C. algae would decrease
D. starfish would show no change

ANALYSIS: To break down material to understand parts

p. 124   AN
A bowling ball is to one complete game of bowling, as a pendulum is to:
A. bob
B. period
C. frequency
D. equilibrium

p. 18   AN
"King of Hearts" is to a deck of cards as cell is to:
A. organ
B. system
C. body
D. tissue

p. 30   AN
Two masses that balance each other on the moon would:
A. be heavier on the moon than on Earth
B. be lighter on the moon than on Earth
C. also balance each other on Earth
D. never balance each other on Earth

SYNTHESIS: To put parts together in a new way

p. 83   S
The following organism is needed to make the food chain complete: green plants ⟶ insects ⟶ frogs ⟶ ?
A. kangaroo
B. cow
C. snake
D. butterfly

p. 80   S
The following stage is needed to complete the life cycle of a grasshopper: egg _?_ adult
A. nymph
B. larva
C. pupa
D. all of the above

p. 86   S
Which of the following is needed to form a complete group: maple, oak, cedar, _____?
A. daisy
B. petunia
C. rose
D. pine

EVALUATION: To make a judgement about the value of materials

p. 116   E
Space vehicles in the future may have electrical power:
A. from solar cells, with parallel wiring
B. from solar cells, with series wiring
C. from dry cells, with parallel wiring
D. from dry cells, with series wiring

p. 2   E
What method would be best for finding out if the moon is really made of green cheese?
A. observation
B. estimation
C. experimentation
D. inference

p. 132   E
One solution to coal, gas and oil shortages is to switch over to electricity. This idea is wrong because:
A. most electricity is produced from coal, gas and oil
B. people will lose their jobs if we switch over to electricity
C. it's impossible to build electric cars in great numbers
D. electricity is too expensive

GA1084

Sample Psychomotor Evaluation

With your hands, some water, ice cubes (glaciers) and rocks, make the following geological features in a large pan of sand. Your features should look like those below. When you have finished making your features, have your teacher check whether you've done them correctly.

Alluvial Fan

Meandering Stream

Oxbow Lake

Delta

Sinkhole

Moraine

Cirque

Drumlin

Erratic

GA1084

Sample Affective Evaluation

For each of the paired items listed below, place an (x) on the line that best represents your feelings about the web experience on _____.

Example: The web on _____ will be (before unit) is (mid-unit) was (end of unit).

	Hot	___	___	___	___	___	___	___	Cold
		(1)	(2)	(3)	(4)	(5)	(6)	(7)	

		(1)	(2)	(3)	(4)	(5)	(6)	(7)	
1.	Interesting	(1)	(2)	(3)	(4)	(5)	(6)	(7)	Boring
2.	Important	(1)	(2)	(3)	(4)	(5)	(6)	(7)	Useless
3.	Informative	(1)	(2)	(3)	(4)	(5)	(6)	(7)	Worthless
4.	Complete	(1)	(2)	(3)	(4)	(5)	(6)	(7)	Incomplete
5.	Mixed Up	(7)	(6)	(5)	(4)	(3)	(2)	(1)	Smooth
6.	A Downer	(7)	(6)	(5)	(4)	(3)	(2)	(1)	An Upper
7.	Selfish	(7)	(6)	(5)	(4)	(3)	(2)	(1)	Unselfish
8.	Enough Time	(1)	(2)	(3)	(4)	(5)	(6)	(7)	Not Enough Time
9.	Light	(1)	(2)	(3)	(4)	(5)	(6)	(7)	Dark
10.	Negative	(7)	(6)	(5)	(4)	(3)	(2)	(1)	Positive
11.	High	(1)	(2)	(3)	(4)	(5)	(6)	(7)	Low
12.	Bad	(7)	(6)	(5)	(4)	(3)	(2)	(1)	Good
13.	Liked	(1)	(2)	(3)	(4)	(5)	(6)	(7)	Disliked
14.	Black	(7)	(6)	(5)	(4)	(3)	(2)	(1)	White
15.	Fast	(1)	(2)	(3)	(4)	(5)	(6)	(7)	Slow

On the other side of this page, list responses to the following:

Things I like(d) best about the web experience.

Things I like(d) least about the web experience.

Suggested changes in the web experience to make it more interesting.

_____ Total Points

(Lower score means more positive experience.)

19

How to Begin the Study of School Yard-Backyard Science

Parent Pages (pages 14 and 15)

Make copies of Tips for Parents. Send tips home to parents. Encourage parents to do Home Activity Pages with youngsters.

Front and Back Covers of Student Book (pages 21 and 22)

Make copies of pages 21 and 22 for each student. Have students cut apart puzzle pieces and put picture together. Glue pieces from page 21 to front and page 22 to back covers of file folder. Have students fill in the blanks with their names and the name of their school. Color. Laminate. Place completed activity and log pages (page 24) in folder. This student book can be taken home each day and becomes a permanent record of all activities done in *School Yard-Backyard Cycles of Science.*

Safety Page (page 23)

Make copies of page 23 for each student. Mount to *inside* of front cover of Student Book. Review all safety rules with students *before* beginning the study of School Yard-Backyard Science.

Activity Pages (pages 25-132)

As needed, make copies of the activity pages in sets of two (school-home) for each student. Even numbered pages, found on the *left* side of the book and designated (S) on the school in upper left corner of each page, are done at school; odd numbered pages, found on the right side of the book and designated (H) on the home in the upper left corner of each page, are done at home. Stress parental involvement in activities done at home to apply what was done in school to a home setting. Activities are *interdisciplinary* and *nonsequential.* Key concepts found in the upper right corner of each page and italicized in the text are defined and cross-referenced in the glossary.

Sequence Strips (pages 25-132)

Many pages feature cards that, when placed in correct order, show a life cycle. Have youngsters cut out cards, place in order and glue to strips of construction paper or cardboard. Put a hole in the end of each strip. Fasten with paper fastener to make a fan-shaped card deck of cycles. Youngsters can also make card decks to show various cycles.

Glossary Pages (pages 143-149)

Make copies of glossary pages for each student. Place in student School Yard-Backyard Science Notebook for easy reference. Have youngsters refer often to the glossary for definitions of key concepts listed in upper left corner on activity pages.

pp. 21-22
Student Book Covers

p. 23
Safety

pp. 25-132
Activity Pages

pp. 14-15
Parent Tips

pp. 25-132
Sequence Strips

pp. 143-149
Glossary

GA1084

21

MY NAME IS _____

My B

ackyard Scie No

I LIVE AT _____

nce tebook

A Student's Guide to Science Safety

Name _____

Because I have the right to be safe in school and at home, I accept the responsibility to:

+ Use patience and common sense when working with science equipment and materials.

+ Report all accidents to the teacher no matter how minor they are or seem to be.

+ Never taste or touch chemicals unless specifically told to do so by my teacher.

+ Roll up long and baggy sleeves above the elbows before doing science activities.

+ Tie long hair behind my head before beginning any science activity.

+ Place newspapers on desks or tables before doing science experiments.

+ Wear old shirts for very messy experiments, but be careful that they are not too baggy.

+ Be alert and proceed with caution when doing science activities.

+ Try not to bump into others. I will go to the learning centers and stay there until all tasks are completed.

+ Do my share to clean up all materials after completing science activities in school and at home.

+ Complete my Master Independent Study Contracts on time and to the best of my ability.

+ Never drink or eat from lab glassware such as bottles and glasses.

+ Never "suck up" a liquid chemical with my mouth.

+ Never sniff or breathe vapors from any gas or chemical.

+ Never point a sharp object or a test tube at anyone or look directly into such a test tube when mixing or heating chemicals.

+ Keep the floor and the centers free of spilled materials.

+ Accept responsibility for the cleaning of science equipment in the classroom.

+ Keep accurate records of my results in my School Yard-Backyard Science Notebook and share these promptly with my teacher and parents.

+ Observe the safety precautions listed and posted by my teacher regarding the use of fire, handling of animals and using electricity.

+ Be the most responsible person that I can possibly be.

+ Attach this page to the inside of the front cover of my School Yard-Backyard Science Notebook and study it frequently.

EXPLOSIVE SUBSTANCES

TOXIC SUBSTANCE

OXIDIZING SUBSTANCE

CORROSIVE SUBSTANCE

FLAMMABLE SUBSTANCE

RADIOACTIVE SUBSTANCE

GA1084

Science Diary and Log

GA1084

Part Two
School Yard (S)-Backyard (B) Earth and Space Science Cycles

Here are some pictures of activities that you and your youngsters will encounter in this section.

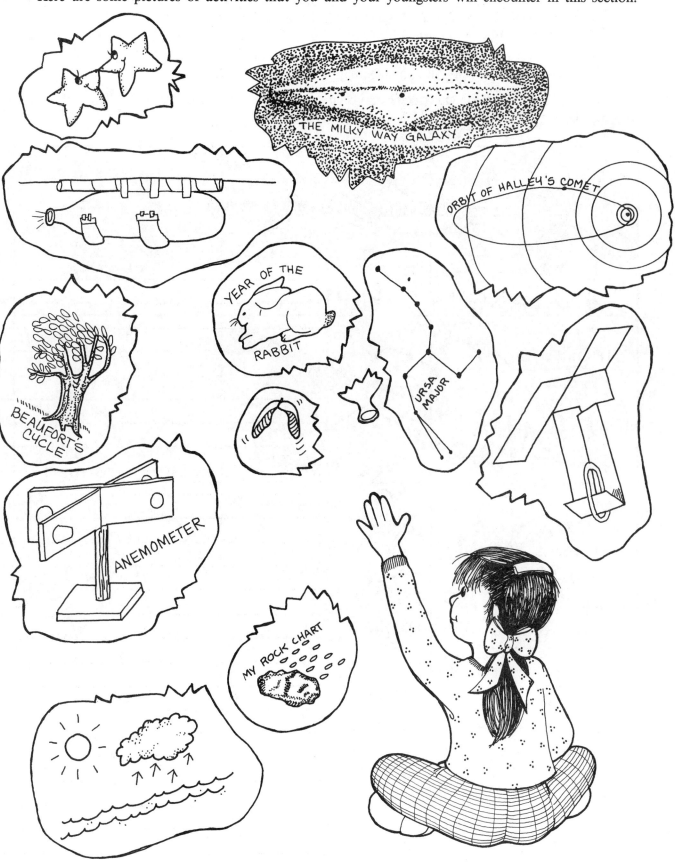

25

Our Universe Is Part of a Long Cycle

COSMOLOGISTS
UNIVERSE

The universe is made up of everything in space and time. COSMOLOGISTS study the origin and structure of the UNIVERSE. You can do the same. Cut apart the cards below. Tape or glue to tagboard or construction paper. Rearrange the squares, in order, to show the history of the UNIVERSE. Put squares on a large chart, showing the correct sequence of events. Find out the approximate time in years that it took for each event to occur. Study its history. Then write a newspaper article on what you think the next big event in history will be.

TIP: Some people think the universe expands and contracts, each cycle taking billions of years to complete.

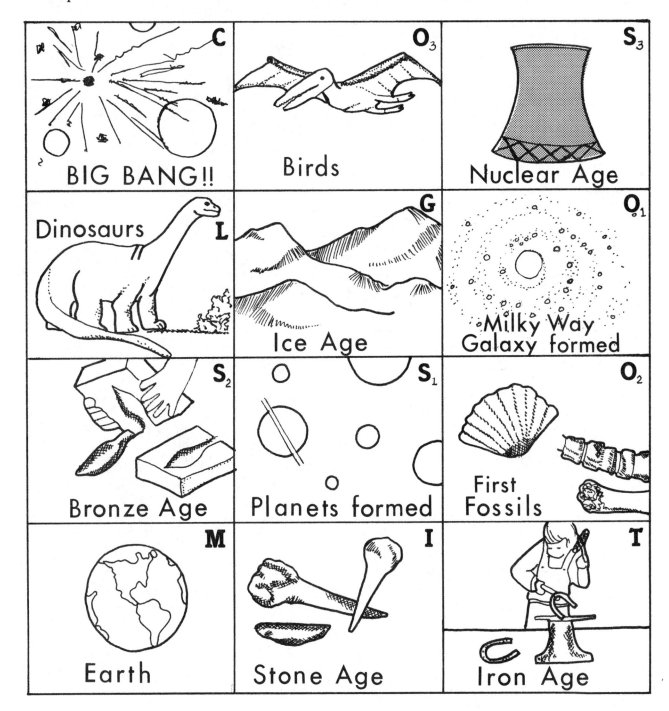

C — BIG BANG!!

O₃ — Birds

S₃ — Nuclear Age

Dinosaurs — L

G — Ice Age

O₁ — Milky Way Galaxy formed

S₂ — Bronze Age

S₁ — Planets formed

O₂ — First Fossils

M — Earth

I — Stone Age

T — Iron Age

GA1084

Our Universe Is a Big Bang

Many scientists believe that long ago all MATTER was a tiny spot. The tiny spot blew apart in a gigantic explosion. MATTER flew out into space. This is called the BIG BANG. Today, scientists believe that the universe is still expanding. Each part is moving away from every other part. Create your own BIG BANG. Cut apart the 23 event cards below. Fold the cards and insert into a balloon. Inflate balloon. Tie. With help from your parents, puncture the balloon with a pin. Note sound and how each piece of paper moves away from every other piece. Compare to BIG BANG. Collect pieces of paper. Tape or glue pieces end to end to make a film. Show often.

TIP: Use paper lunch bag instead of the balloon.

Our Galaxy Is a Spiral Cycle

A GALAXY is a huge cluster of stars. There are billions of GALAXIES in the universe. Our GALAXY, the MILKY WAY GALAXY, is one such GALAXY. Below is a picture of the MILKY WAY GALAXY. It is shaped like a spiral. It has many stars. In Figure 1, the sun's position is marked with an "X." The center of the galaxy is marked with a "C." Use the scale of light-years below to answer the questions. Then mount the picture of the GALAXY on black construction paper. Punch hole through page at sun's location. Tape to clear window for all to view.

TIP: Tape red or yellow cellophane paper over hole to make the color of our sun. View often. Then cut out the spiral galaxy in Figure 2. Compare to spiral shape of the MILKY WAY GALAXY.

TIP: The Milky Way completes one rotation every 200 million years.

Figure 1: MILKY WAY GALAXY

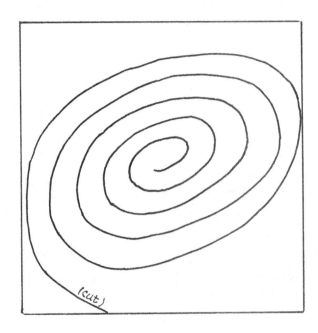

Figure 2: With scissors, cut on solid black line above to make your own spiral GALAXY.

QUESTIONS:

1. How far in light-years does our sun lie from the center of the MILKY WAY GALAXY? _____

2. Approximately how far in light-years is it across the MILKY WAY GALAXY?_____

Scale of Light-Years
1″ = Approximately 33,000 light-years 2.5 cm = Approximately 33,000 light-years

28

GA1084

Our Galaxy Is a Milky Way

Scientists believe that our galaxy may look something like this:

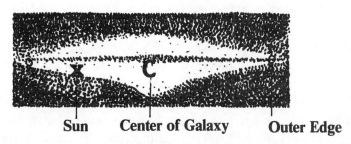

Sun   Center of Galaxy   Outer Edge

The sun, shown at point "X," lies about 33,000 LIGHT-YEARS from the center (point C) of the galaxy. Make your own Milky Way Galaxy by taping two 9-inch (23 cm) pie plates together like this:

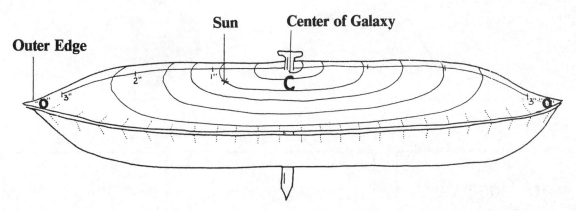

With a nail, poke a hole through the center of both plates. Label this point C the center of the Milky Way Galaxy. Cut out the mini snack bar below. Starting at point C, measure a 3-inch (7.5 cm) line two snack bars long to the left of C. Poke a hole through the two plates at the end of the line. Label this point O, the outer edge of the galaxy. Do the same 3-inch (7.5 cm) line to the right of point C. Starting at point C, draw a 1-inch (2.5 cm) line to the left of point C. Punch a hole through both plates at the end of the line. Label this point X, our sun. Then answer these questions.

1. How many mini snack bars is it from the center of the galaxy to the outer edge of the galaxy? ____

2. If one mini snack bar (1.5 inches) represents 25,000 LIGHT-YEARS, how many light-years is it from the center of the galaxy to its outer edge? _____

3. If the distance from the center of the galaxy to the sun is .75 mini snack bars, or 1 inch (2.5 cm), how many LIGHT-YEARS is it from the center of the galaxy to the sun? _____

4. If your mini snack bar is .5 inch (1.25 cm) thick, how many LIGHT-YEARS thick is your galaxy? _____

Decorate your galaxy with spirals. Twirl your galaxy on the nail for all to see.

GA1084

Life Cycle of a Star

Scientists believe the life of a star begins when a huge cloud of dust and gas particles collect together. Gravity pulls the gases together to form a solid mass. Heat is produced. The young star begins to grow. It shines for millions of years. As time passes, the fuel in its core is used up. The star turns into a RED GIANT. Finally, the RED GIANT loses its outer layers and becomes a small, very dense WHITE DWARF star. Eventually, the WHITE DWARF star slowly cools until it looks like a cinder in space. Our sun is not big enough to explode as a SUPERNOVA but some bigger stars can. The life cycle of a supergiant is much the same but even more spectacular. Study the life cycle of a SUPERNOVA by cutting out the cards below. Make a deck of cards. Rearrange cards in order, to show the star's life cycle. Mix up cards. Have a friend stack the deck in order. Then study the Crab Nebula in the constellation Taurus. The Crab Nebula is the remains of a star that blew up into a SUPERNOVA in the year 1054.

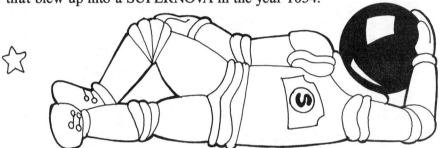

Red Supergiant is out of fuel. OH! OH! **R**	The very massive neutron star may become a black hole. **A**	Matter condenses to form a blue supergiant. **U**
Life begins for a supergiant well within a nebula which is made up of many distant stars. **S**	The outer layers of the supergiant cool. The blue supergiant becomes a red supergiant. **E**	After squashed by gravity, supergiant fights back outward as a beautiful supernova. **O**
The remains of a supernova form a very dense core called a neutron star. **V**	Gravity squashes red supergiant. UGH! **N**	Supergiant uses up hydrogen, combines with heavier substances and expands 10 times in size. **P**

GA1084

Our Sun's Cycle: from Hot to Cold

Our sun is a star in the Milky Way Galaxy. Although very hot, our sun is a star of average temperature when compared to other stars. The temperatures of stars range from "O" stars, the hottest, to "M" stars, the coolest. Below is a picture of our sun. The letters O B A F G K M are found at the bottom of the page. These letters stand for various temperatures of stars. Using an encyclopedia, find out the temperature of our sun. Cut out the correct letter below that stands for our sun's temperature. Paste the letter in the core of the sun. Fill in the blanks below the core.

TIPS: A peak in solar activity in the form of sunspots and solar flares occurs every eleven years. A sunbeam, the time it takes a beam of light to travel from the sun to the earth, has a life span of 8.3 minutes.

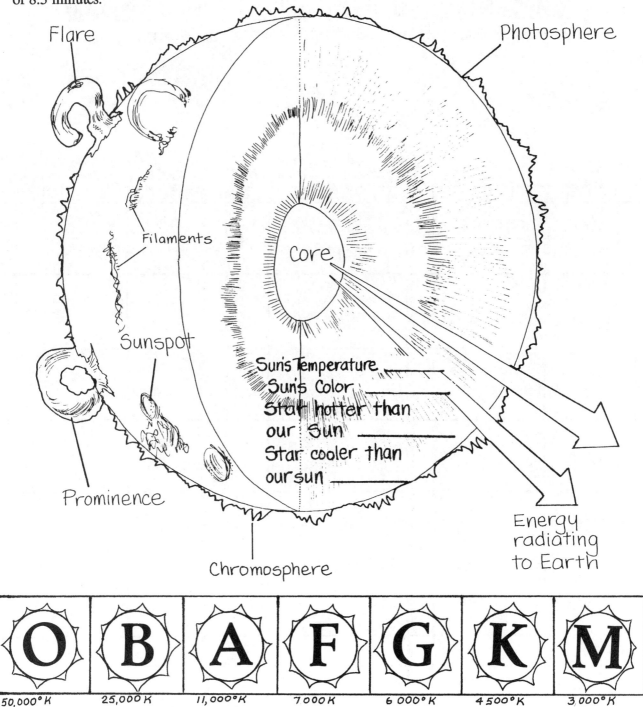

Flare

Photosphere

Filaments

Core

Sun's Temperature _____
Sun's Color _____
Star hotter than
our Sun _____
Star cooler than
our sun _____

Sunspot

Prominence

Chromosphere

Energy radiating to Earth

O	B	A	F	G	K	M
50,000°K	25,000 K	11,000°K	7000 K	6 000°K	4 500°K	3 000°K

31

GA1084

Temperature Cycles of Stars

Billions of stars make up millions of galaxies. Stars are classified according to their temperatures. You can study this by knowing the letters O B A F G K M, which mean "Oh, Be A Fine Girl Kiss Me." "O" stars are the hottest, "M" stars are the coolest. "O" stars are blue in color, "M" stars are red. Complete the chart below. The first one is done for you.

TIP: Further subdivisions in the classification of stars exist. The subdivisions of the O B A F G K M groups are shown by a number after the letter, such as O1-O9, B1-B9. Our sun is a G2 star, which means that when one examines the light given off by the sun, its rich atomic spectrum has a large number of lines of iron and other neutral elements.

"As astronomers, we use the KELVIN TEMPERATURE SCALE."

Word in Saying	Class	Example	Approximate Temperature	Color
"Oh	O5	No Bright Star	50,000° K	Blue-White
Be				
A				
Fine				
Girl				
Kiss				
Me"				

GA1084

Daily Cycles of Stars

Supergiant stars go through a *life* cycle that takes millions of years. Some stars, however, go through a *traveling* cycle that takes only one day. These stars are called CIRCUMPOLAR stars. They never rise or set. They complete a daily cycle as they circle the pole star, POLARIS. Below is a picture of CIRCUMPOLAR stars. The large circle has CIRCUMPOLAR stars that can be seen if you live at about 40⁰ north latitude. Take this page outside each night at the same time. Face *north*. Hold page slightly upward. Turn page so that POLARIS, the North Star, lines up with POLARIS in the sky. Then find the following: Ursa Major, Ursa Minor and Cassiopeia. Note time. Line up a familiar landmark, such as the top of a pole, with the Big Dipper. Mark a spot on the ground where you are standing. Return to your position the following week at the same time. Observe the position of the Big Dipper relative to the pole. Describe its location. Make a drawing of the location of other stars in the sky. Find out how long it took the stars to complete their cycles around POLARIS. Then study the picture of STAR TRAILS below. The photograph shows the paths of stars as they travel around POLARIS, the North Star. With chalk, draw some circumpolar stars on black construction paper. Display for all to see.

LYRA
Vega
PRECESSION CIRCLE
CYGNUS
Deneb
DRACO
URSA MINOR
CEPHEUS
URSA MAJOR
Polaris
CASSIOPEIA
CAMELOPARDALIS
+40°
Capella
AURIGA

Photograph of Star Trails

33

GA1084

Timing Planetary Cycles

Our solar system has nine PLANETS, their moons and other small bodies. All these cycle around our star, the sun, in elliptical ORBITS. Below is a picture of our sun and nine PLANETS. Name each PLANET by writing its name in the blank. Find out how long it takes each PLANET to cycle around the sun. Write your answer in the blank. Then answer the challenge questions below.

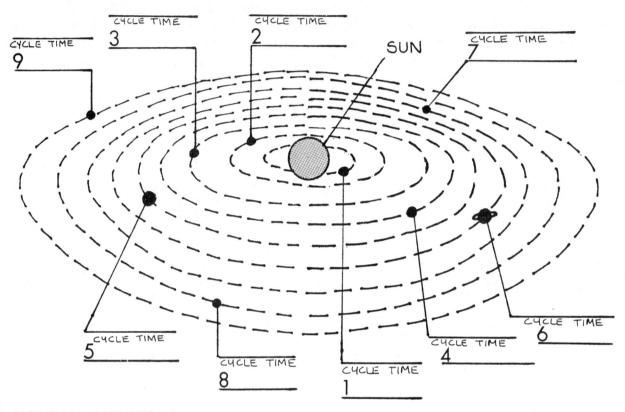

CHALLENGE QUESTIONS:

1. Which planet has liquid water? _____
2. Which planet is all desert? _____
3. Which planet is similar to a greenhouse? _____
4. Which planet is the red planet? _____
5. Which planet has the shortest day? _____
6. Which planet could float in water? _____
7. Which planet has the longest winter? _____
8. Which planets are called "The Twins"? _____
9. Which is the smallest planet? _____
10. William Herschel lived to age 84. Which planet takes 84 years to cycle around the sun? Herschel discovered this planet._____
11. Which planet is the farthest from the sun until the year 1999? _____
12. How many years would it take a jogger to jog around Jupiter? _____
13. If you lived on Pluto, how many years would you have to wait for your first birthday?_____
14. If you lived on Mercury, how many birthdays would you have per year? _____

GA1084

Planetary Cycles: Largest to Smallest

Some scientists believe that many years ago our sun, earth and planets were a cloud of cold dust particles in empty space. Gradually, the particles came together to form a huge, spinning DISK. As it spun, the DISK became hot. The center of the DISK became the sun. The planets were made from fiery gases and liquid matter near the sun. Our earth, a huge ball of rock, is one of these planets. Below is a picture of our solar system. Attach page to a strong piece of cardboard. Find a rock or tiny pebble that matches the size of each planet. Line up rocks according to *size*. Which planet is the largest? Smallest? Record your findings in the chart below. The first one is done for you. Tape rocks to matching planets on the cardboard. Then with a pair of binoculars, observe at least one planet tonight. Report what you saw to members of your family.

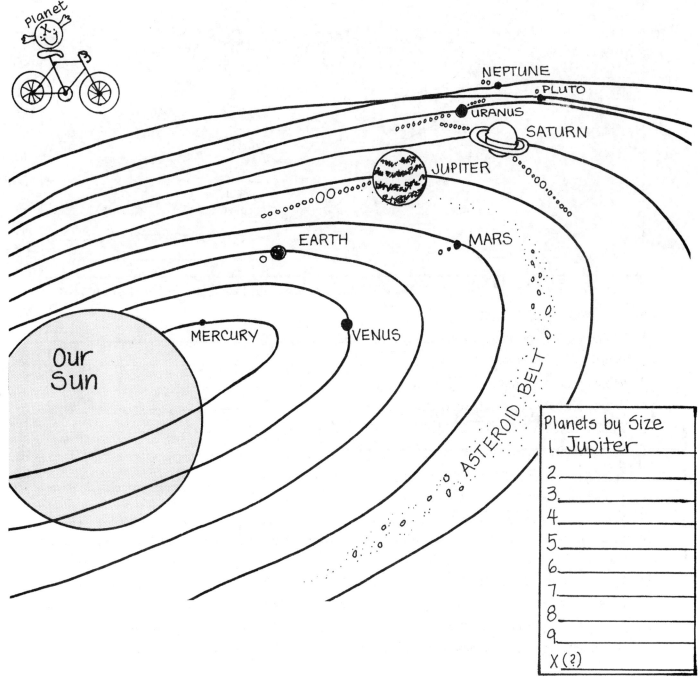

Planets by Size
1. Jupiter
2.
3.
4.
5.
6.
7.
8.
9.
X (?)

35

Halley's Comet: a 76-Year Cycle

A COMET is like a dusty snowball that races around the sun. Halley's Comet is the most famous of all comets. The Chinese observed Halley's Comet in 240 B.C. Since then, Comet Halley has repeated its cycle about every 76 years, the last time being in 1986. Recreate this historical event. Below is a picture of the path Comet Halley took in 1986. Cut out the comet. Place on start, November 1. Move comet along path. End at May 1. Fill in the chart below. Pretend that you are Comet Halley. Make a tape recording of what you might see on your voyage around the sun. Be sure to include information on when you will return.

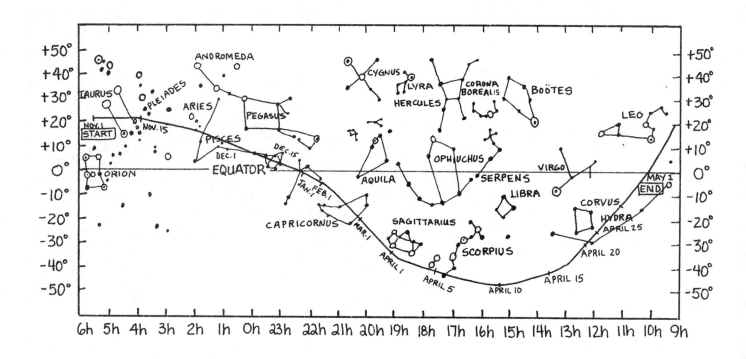

DATE	NEAREST CONSTELLATION
Nov. 15	
Dec. 1	
	Crosses Equator for First Time
March 1	
April 1	
April 5	
April 25	
	Crosses Equator for Second Time

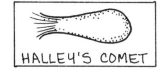

HALLEY'S COMET

36

GA1084

Comet Halley Flip Book: a 76-Year Rerun

Before movies were made, people made it look like pictures were moving. They did this by taking many slightly different pictures and stapling them together. When one flipped the pictures quickly, objects in the pictures appeared to move. You can see Comet Halley move by making a flip book. Cut out the cards below. Glue to stiff cardboard with number one on top. With your right thumb on top, flip through the cards. Write a book about Comet Halley. Be sure to include a drawing of its three parts—NUCLEUS, COMA and TAIL—in the book. Color the comet.

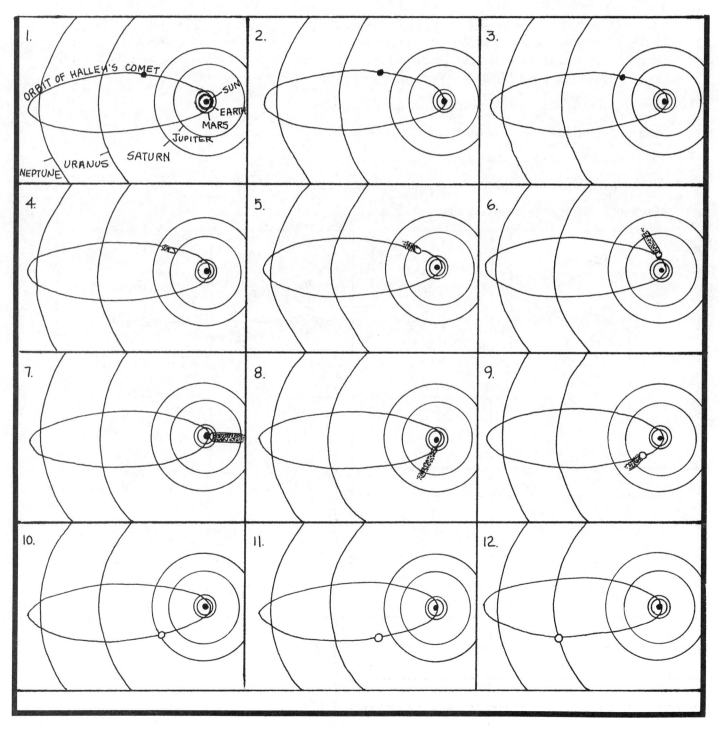

Just for Fun:
Twelve-Year Eastern World Zodiac Cycle

The Eastern World ZODIAC is based on a twelve-year cycle, each year shown by an animal. Below are pictures of twelve such animals. These animals supposedly lined up to say good-bye to Buddha as he lay on his deathbed. Under the appropriate picture, circle the year in which you were born. In the blanks, write your year, sign and personality traits. If you were born in 1970, the year of the dog, your personality trait would be that of a "loyal" person. Other words to choose from: RAT—works hard, OX—patient, TIGER—deep thinker, RABBIT—ambitious, DRAGON—honest, SNAKE—sensitive, HORSE—cheerful, SHEEP—wise, MONKEY—clever, ROOSTER—deep thinker, DOG—loyal, BOAR—kind. When finished, make an Eastern World ZODIAC scrapbook. Note the year of birth, sign and personality traits of at least twelve of your friends. Compare them to famous people whose names are listed below each picture. What traits do they have in common? Include information about yourself in the scrapbook.

I was born in Western World year 19 _____.

According to Eastern World calendar, I was born in the year _____.

My Eastern World sign is that of a(n) _____.

My Eastern World personality trait(s) is(are) _____.

Name of famous person with my sign _____.

RAT
(Churchill, Washington)
1972, 1984
(4670) (4682)

OX
(Walt Disney, Van Gogh)
1973, 1985
(4671) (4683)

TIGER
(Marco Polo, Marilyn Monroe)
1974, 1986
(4672) (4684)

RABBIT
(Confucius, Einstein)
1975, 1987
(4673) (4685)

DRAGON
(Joan of Arc, Freud)
1976, 1988
(4674) (4686)

SNAKE
(Darwin, Lincoln)
1977, 1989
(4675) (4687)

HORSE
(Rembrandt, Davy Crockett)
1966, 1978
(4664) (4676)

SHEEP
(Michaelangelo, Orville Wright)
1967, 1979
(4665) (4677)

MONKEY
(Julius Caesar, Elizabeth Taylor)
1968, 1980
(4666) (4678)

ROOSTER
(Rudyard Kipling, Caruso)
1969, 1981
(4667) (4679)

DOG
(Socrates, Benjamin Franklin)
1970, 1982
(4668) (4680)

BOAR
(Albert Schweitzer, Ernest Hemingway)
1971, 1983
(4669) (4681)

GA1084

Just for Fun:
One-Year Western World Zodiac Cycle

Youngsters think about "far out" things in space. They are interested in space. Thoughts often turn to ASTROLOGY because it is fun to study. Below is a picture of the Western World yearly zodiac cycle, a circle of animals that shows the path of the moon and earth as they revolve around the sun. In your notebook, list, then learn the name of each zodiac sign. Then complete the activities in the boxes below. When completed, make a display that shows the zodiac sign for each of your family members. Color each sign.

Write the date of your birthday here.

Draw and label the figure that represents your zodiac sign here.

Draw the symbol for your zodiac sign here.

List today's date here.

Clip your HOROSCOPE from today's newspaper and paste it here.

In this box, write your reaction to the statement that your HOROSCOPE can foretell your future.

GA1084

Meteorites: a Yearly Cycle of Showers

A METEOROID is a solid object that moves rapidly through space. As it enters the earth's atmosphere it appears as a bright glowing streak. These streaks are often called "shooting stars" or METEORITES. Below is a chart with the names of nine yearly meteor showers. Look at the pictures below. Color each. In the column on the right, write the *number* of the constellation in which the meteor shower can be seen. Then solve the riddle, "Why did Ann Hodges wake up with a severe headache one morning in 1954?" Answer on page 141.

Important Monthly Meteor Showers

Meteor Shower Name	Begins	Maximum	Ends	Location and Position of Radiant	Number
Quandrantids	1/1	1/3	January 6	Northern Bootes	
Lyrids	4/9	4/22	April 24	Hercules	
Eta Aquarids	5/2	5/4	May 7	Aquarius	
Delta Aquarids	7/15	7/28	August 15	Aquarius	
Perseids	7/25	8/12*	August 18	Cassiopeia	
Orionids	10/16	10/21	October 26	Northern Orion	
Leonids	11/15	11/17*	November 19	Leo	
Geminids	12/7	12/14*	December 15	Gemini	
Ursids	12/17	12/22	December 24	Ursa Minor	

*Be sure to see these; they are brilliant.

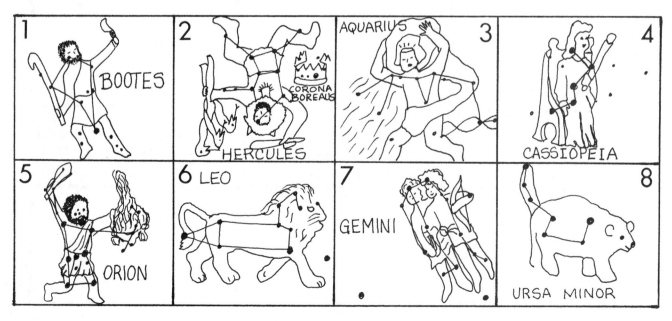

Meteorites:
Photographing a Yearly Cycle of Showers

Meteor showers occur throughout the year. The challenge is to capture them on film. Look at the chart on page 40 to learn when meteor showers occur. Go outside and locate the constellation from which the meteor shower will come. Your best bet is when the RADIANT (point in the sky from which the meteor appears to come) is high overhead. Aim your camera slightly away from the RADIANT. Open the shutter. If after several minutes a meteor has not crossed through the view of your camera, stop the exposure and start again. If nearby lights brighten the sky, use a shorter exposure time. When a meteor is seen by the camera, stop the exposure, advance the film, aim the camera in a different part of the sky and try again. Lie back and enjoy the celestial fireworks. In some meteor showers, you can see up to 50 meteorites in one hour.

TIP: If you are unable to view a meteor shower, you can make things glow in the dark like a meteorite. Purchase some wintergreen Life Savers and some Curad bandages. First, sit in a dark room like your bathroom for 15 minutes. Then chew rapidly on a Life Saver. Watch the fireworks come from your mouth. Open a Curad bandage wrapper. Observe. Try to find out more about what causes this celestial fireworks. Then draw your own meteor shower.

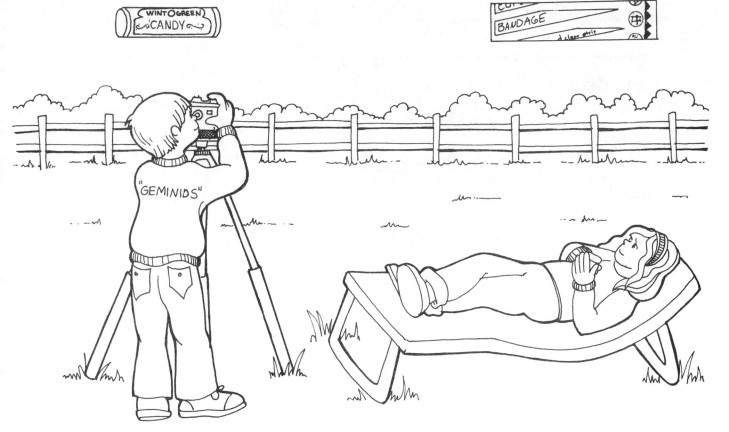

Analemma:
Our Sun's Apparent Yearly Cycle

ANALEMMA
LATITUDE
EQUATOR
TROPIC OF CANCER
TROPIC OF
CAPRICORN

The ANALEMMA shows the position of the sun and its LATITUDE every day of the year. It looks like a figure 8. You can find it on a globe or sundial. In the boxes, write an "X" on the EQUATOR, a "Y" on the TROPIC OF CANCER, a "Z" on the TROPIC OF CAPRICORN. Circle September 21st and March 21st. The sun at noon is directly overhead at the EQUATOR on these days. Circle June 21st. On this day the sun is directly overhead at the TROPIC OF CANCER. For people in the Northern Hemisphere, this is the *longest* period of daylight during the year. Circle December 21st. The sun is directly overhead at the TROPIC OF CAPRICORN. This is the *shortest* period of daylight for people in the Northern Hemisphere. Cut out the figure. Mount on thick cardboard. Push pins into today's date and that of your birthday. Read the latitude at which the sun is located on these days. Decide whether you will have more or less daylight hours on these days than you had yesterday. Then move the pin daily as each day passes by.

Today's Date:

_____

My Birthday:

_____

My birthday will have:

   more   less

daylight   hours than today.

Season in which birthday occurs:

  SPRING

  SUMMER

  FALL

  WINTER

THE ANALEMMA

42

Our Sun's Apparent Seasonal Yearly Cycle

DAYLIGHT

At home, mount this analemma on a thick piece of cardboard, corkboard or on the bulletin board. Push pin into board at today's date. Decide whether the day is a day of long or short hours of DAYLIGHT. With help from family members, look in the newspaper or almanac to find the number of hours and minutes of daylight for that day. Record these findings in your Backyard Science Notebook. Then look at how high the sun is located in the sky. What does this tell you about the season of the year? Move pin as each day passes. Note changes in the number of hours and minutes of daylight and compare to the location of the sun in the sky. During which seasons do you have the most and least number of hours and minutes of daylight? Is the sun low or high in the sky during these seasons? Write your answers in your Backyard Science Notebook. Then color the spring part of the analemma green; summer, yellow; fall, brown; and winter leave white.

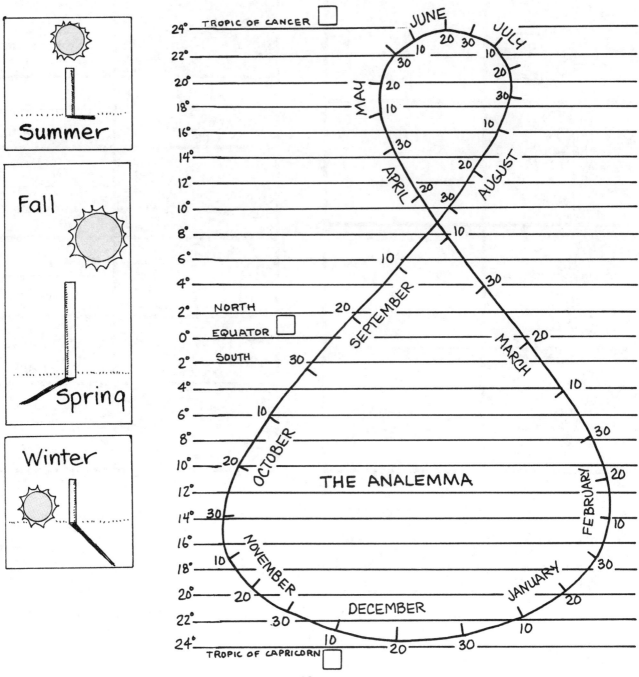

Our Seasons: a Yearly Cycle

Many youngsters know there are four basic seasons: spring, summer, fall and winter. Another way to learn the cycle of seasons, however, is to divide the year into six seasons. In Chart A below, write the name of each season next to the matching picture. In Chart B, write the names of the six matching seasons. Words to choose from—Chart A: Spring, Summer Winter, Fall. Chart B: prevernal, VERNAL, aestival, serotinal, AUTUMNAL, hibernal or hiemal. Color each season. Then using a farmer's almanac, answer the questions below.

TIP: The seasons complete an annual cycle as the tilted earth revolves around the sun in a slightly elliptical orbit.

A Yearly Cycle of Four Seasons
Chart A

A Yearly Cycle of Six Seasons
Chart B

(Early spring)

(Late spring)

(Early summer)

(Late summer)

(Fall)

or

(Winter)

QUESTIONS:

On what date in the yearly cycle of seasons does the *vernal equinox* (first day of spring) occur? _____

On what date does the *autumnal equinox* (first day of fall) occur? _____

On what date in the yearly cycle of the seasons does the *summer solstice* (first day of summer) occur? _____

On what date in the yearly cycle of the seasons does the *winter solstice* (first day of winter) occur?

_____

GA1084

Our Seasons:
a Cycle of Yearly Change

With four sticks and a piece of string two yards (2 meters) long, stake out two-square yards (meters) of land surrounding a tree. Adopt this two-square yards (meters) of land to study during the four seasons of the year. Observe your plot of land at each of four levels shown below: first on your stomach, then on your back. On a piece of paper, make a chart like the one below. Record changes seen at each level during each season of the year, for example, number of creatures, soil and air TEMPERATURES, changes in the tree, clouds and CONSTELLATIONS. Attach to refrigerator door or bedroom window as a reminder to do your observations monthly.

	Spring	Summer	Fall	Winter
Sky:				
Tree Level:				
Ground Level:				
Underground:				

GA1084

Study Our Moon's Monthly Cycle

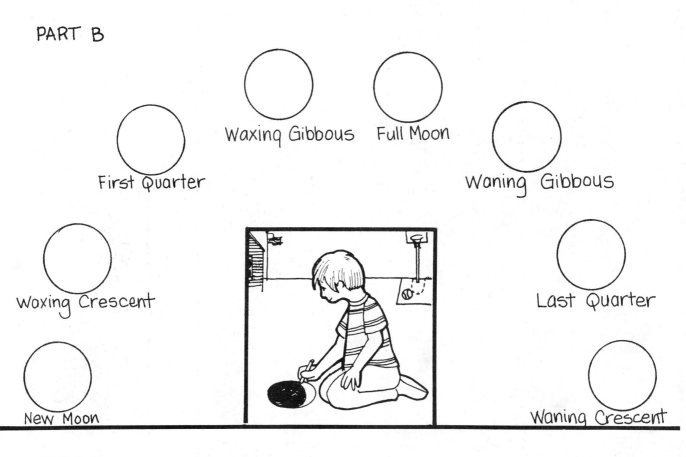

Cut out the eight PHASES of the moon in Part A below. Glue or tape these PHASES to the matching circles on the playground, Part B, below. Using white cardboard and markers, make your own eight PHASES of the moon. Put them in order from new moon to waning CRESCENT. Then in your notebook, list the phases of the moon that you can see anytime from dawn to dusk.

TIP: The cycle from full moon to full moon takes 29.5 days. This period is called the synodical month.

PART B

First Quarter   Waxing Gibbous   Full Moon   Waning Gibbous

Waxing Crescent   Last Quarter

New Moon   Waning Crescent

PART A

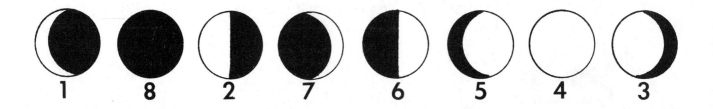

1   8   2   7   6   5   4   3

46   GA1084

Observe Our Moon's Monthly Cycle

Go outside tonight and observe the moon. Draw a picture of today's moon phase in Box 1. Draw a picture in Box 2 of how you feel while observing the moon. Draw a picture of what you think tomorrow's moon phase will be in Box 3. Find other objects in the sky. Identify each. Tomorrow night, observe the moon again at the same time. Find out if yesterday's prediction of the phase of the moon in Box 3 was correct. Then look for changes in the sky that occurred from day one to day two. Make a record of those changes in your *Backyard Science Notebook.*

TIP: The white parts on the moons below are the parts lit up by the sun; the black parts have little or no light reflected from the surface.

TIP: A moonbeam, light from the sun reflected off the moon, takes 1.3 seconds to travel from the moon to the earth.

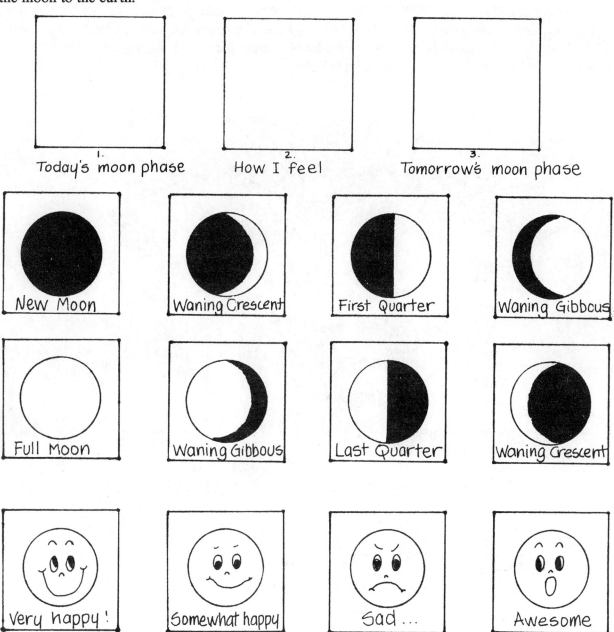

"I have no doubt the moon has an effect on human behavior." Carl Sagan

47

GA1084

Stonehenge: a Seasonal, Daily Cycle

HEELSTONE
GNOMON
TRILITHON
LENTIL

Before watches were made, people told time by looking at the sky. They observed that certain events occurred in regular cycles such as sunrise to sunset and spring, summer, fall and winter. By keeping accurate records, people found out the longest and shortest days of the year.

In Southern England, people built a monument called Stonehenge. It has huge stones up to 36 feet (12 meters) tall. Stonehenge may have been used as a calendar to show the cycles of the seasons, eclipses and the longest and shortest days of the year. In the drawing of Stonehenge below, the sun rises in the east. Its rays strike a HEELSTONE called a GNOMON. On June 21st, the HEELSTONE casts a shadow in the center of Stonehenge. By observing this, people learned that June 21st was the longest day of the year. Soon thereafter, the sun would rise farther south and the shadow was *shorter*, thus the people knew that fall was approaching. Study Stonehenge below. Measure the shadow cast by the HEELSTONE to the nearest inch (cm). Print the words SUN, HEELSTONE, LENTIL and TRILITHON in the matching blanks on the chart. Use your glossary to find out what these words mean. Then study this amazing fact: One stone at Stonehenge equals 37,200 bricks. Using these bricks, you could build a one brick thick chimney 12 feet (4 m) in diameter and 186 feet (62 m) tall. That's a big chimney.

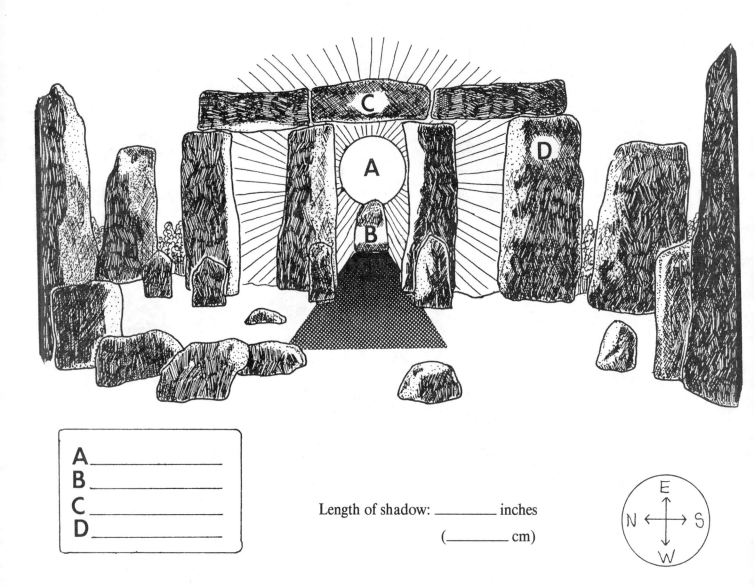

A _____
B _____
C _____
D _____

Length of shadow: _____ inches

(_____ cm)

48

Sundial: a Seasonal, Daily Cycle

Observe regular cycles of SUNRISE to SUNSET and the seasons with a sundial. You will need a large piece of plywood, plastic or single-layered cardboard, stick or dowel, clay, erasable marking pen, paper clips, and clear Con-Tact paper. Obtain a large sheet of plywood, plastic or single-layered cardboard. Refrigerator boxes work well for this. Cover with clear Con-Tact paper. Cut a hole or put a piece of clay in the center of the sheet. Insert dowel or stick into hole or clay so it is upright. With erasable pen, write N, S, E and W near four edges of cardboard. Go outside. Orient sundial with "S" facing south. At 30-minute intervals, draw the sun's shadow on the cardboard or plastic. Draw lines using erasable felt-tipped pens. Mark the end of the shadow with a paper clip or pebble. Measure the length of the sun's shadow every 30 minutes. Note directions (E, W, N, S) in which the shadow appears. Note season of year and location of shadow. Reuse sundial often by wiping off pen marks with damp cloth or paper towel. Compare your sundial to that of Stonehenge.

TIP: Never look directly at the sun. Youngsters can roll out adding machine tape that matches the length of the sun's shadow. Record time of day and season on each strip of adding machine tape. Post on wall in your home for all to see. Discuss the lengths of strips of adding machine tape for various times of the day and seasons of the year. At which time of the day is the sun's shadow the longest? Shortest? Be sure to do this during each season of the year. Does the length of the sun's shadow differ for each season? Record your findings in your Backyard Science Notebook.

TIP: The earth rotates on its axis once a day. The solar day is 24 hours, from sunrise to sunrise.

GA1084

Time: a Daily Cycle

Before watches were made, people observed the location of the stars to tell time. You can do the same. In school, prepare for your nighttime mission of telling the correct time to the nearest half hour using the stars. Below is a picture of a large clock. For your **night** observation, you will need to know the names of familiar constellations. Fill in the blanks with the names of these five constellations: Cassiopeia, Cepheus, Draco, Big Dipper and Little Dipper. With your finger, follow the line from POLARIS to the Pointer Stars. You will need to locate these in the sky tonight. You are now ready for your night observation. Your mission is to find the correct time without using a watch. Good luck in your mission.

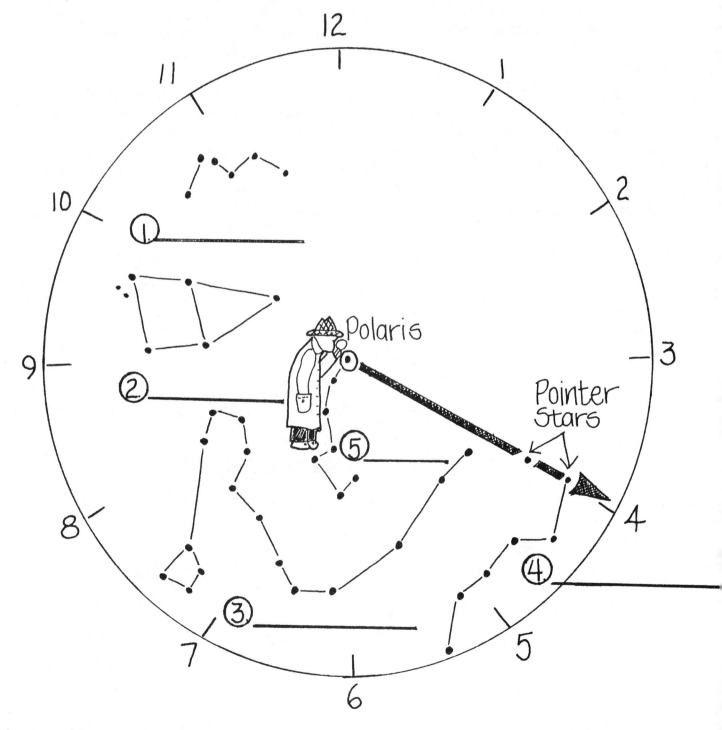

GA1084

Time: a Daily Nighttime Cycle

Telling TIME by the stars has been a common practice for many ancient civilizations. It has only been since watches were made that we moved away from using the stars to tell TIME.

With practice you can tell the correct TIME within one half hour without using a watch. Stand outside on a clear night. Find the BIG DIPPER and the North Star, Polaris. Imagine that Polaris is at the center of a large clock and that the two pointer stars of the BIG DIPPER are the hour hand of the clock. An arrow drawn through the pointer stars directed away from Polaris will point to the time on your imaginary clock. Read the time to the nearest hour. For a more accurate result, read the time to the nearest half hour. To that time, add the number of *months* that have passed since the first of January. Do not forget to add any fraction of a month. Double the number you now have and subtract it from 16.25 or 40.25, whichever will give you a positive result. Your final answer will be the approximate time. So you can tell the time at night by merely looking to the sky. Share this technique with your friends and family members. Congratulations, mission accomplished.

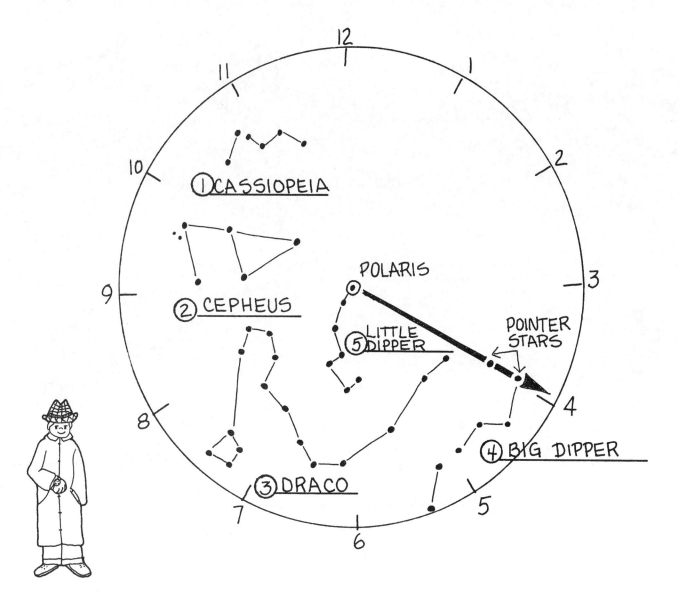

Cycling Around the World in 9 Days— Without Refueling

In December 1986, Dick Rutan and Jeana Yeager on board *Voyager* made a complete cycle around the world without refueling. It was an important accomplishment in aviation history. Pretend that the point on your pencil is *Voyager*. Place it on "start." Connect the dots going westward toward Hawaii to show the route that *Voyager* traveled. Fill in the blanks below with correct information gathered from your travels. Then use your glossary to find out what the words LIFT, THRUST, DRAG and GRAVITY mean.

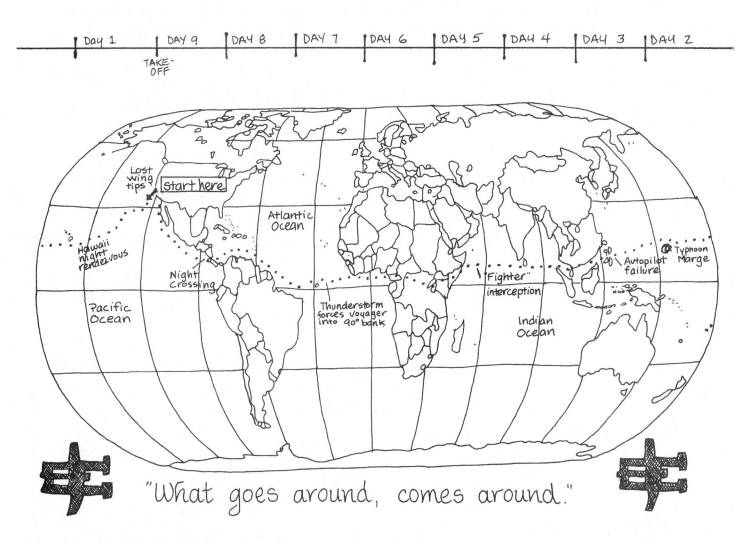

1. On what day did *Voyager* lose its wingtips?_____

2. On what day did *Voyager* meet Typhoon Marge?_____

3. On what day did *Voyager* experience autopilot failure?_____

4. On what day did a thunderstorm force *Voyager* into a 90⁰ bank?_____

5. Over what Central American country did *Voyager* make a night crossing?_____

6. How many days did it take *Voyager* to make one complete cycle of the earth?_____

52

GA1084

A Dry Run: Flying Full Cycle— Without Fuel

Get a feel for flying by building an airplane. First you will need to know its parts.

Write the number in the blank that best identifies

that part of the airplane, _____ Right AILERON,

_____ Right Wing, _____ Cowling, _____ Spinner,

_____ Propeller, _____ Nose Gear, _____ Engine,

_____ Landing Gear, _____ Left Wing,

_____ Left Aileron, _____ Landing FLAP,

_____ Fuselage, _____ Horizontal

Stabilizer, _____ Elevator, _____ Vertical

Stabilizer, _____ RUDDER.

Use this pattern to make your airplane. Fly many flights. Then read information in Columns B, C, D and E. Fill in Column A with what you think the response of your plane will be. Your choices are "climb" and "dive." Then fly your plane to find out if you were correct.

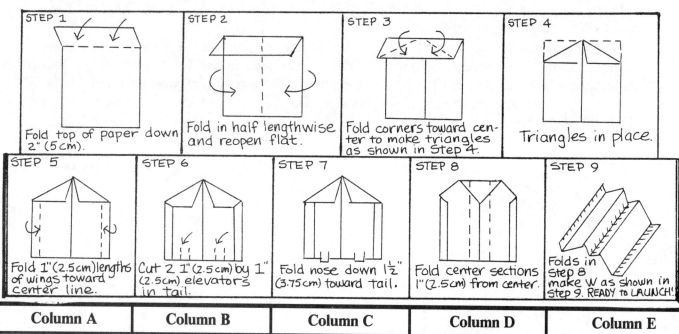

STEP 1	STEP 2	STEP 3	STEP 4
Fold top of paper down 2" (5cm).	Fold in half lengthwise and reopen flat.	Fold corners toward center to make triangles as shown in Step 4.	Triangles in place.

STEP 5	STEP 6	STEP 7	STEP 8	STEP 9
Fold 1"(2.5cm)lengths of wings toward center line.	Cut 2 1"(2.5cm) by 1" (2.5cm) elevators in tail.	Fold nose down 1½" (3.75cm) toward tail.	Fold center sections 1"(2.5cm) from center.	Folds in step 8 make W as shown in step 9. READY to LAUNCH!

Column A	Column B		Column C	Column D	Column E
I think the airplane will (climb or dive).	The ailerons go up or down or remain flat.		The flaps go down or remain flat.	The elevator goes up, down, or remains flat.	The rudder is straight or goes left, right.
	Left	Right			
1. _____	flat	flat	flat	up	straight
2. _____	flat	flat	down	up	straight

GA1084

Spinning Cycles:
Counterclockwise or Clockwise

A helicopter can go straight up, straight down, backward, forward, sideways or can stay in one spot and turn completely around. The rotor blades make many cycles in one minute.

Using the drawing below, write the number in the blank that best matches that part of the helicopter. (_____) tail rotor, (_____) tail boom, (_____) landing gear, (_____) engine, (_____) controls, (_____) cockpit, (_____) main rotor, (_____) rotor hub, (_____) mast and (_____) drive shaft. Then call members of an airplane company or flight school. Try to find out if a helicopter's main rotor turns clockwise or counterclockwise and what happens when you change the PITCH of its blades.

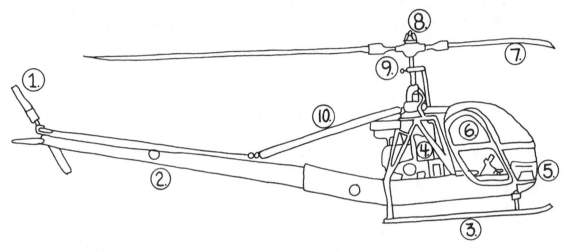

On the playground, find a maple seed. It is oval-shaped and looks like the one in Figure A. Gently drop the maple seed to the ground. Observe. Cut seed in half lengthwise. Drop. Observe the direction in which the seed twirls. Compare this to the direction in which the main rotor of a helicopter turns. Are they the same or different? Do they spin clockwise or counterclockwise? Fill in the blanks below.

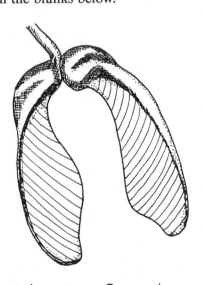

Maple Seed

Figure A

Figure B

Movements: _____

Clockwise_____

Counterclockwise_____

54

GA1084

Spinning Cycles: Helicopter

ROTOR
CLOCKWISE
COUNTERCLOCK-
WISE

Make and fly your own helicopter. Read these directions carefully and you will be ready for your first test flight.

DIRECTIONS: Cut rectangular shape on solid black lines. Cut on dotted lines D, E and F. Fold *flaps* A and C over flap B and add paper clip. Bend ROTOR Blade A away from ROTOR Blade B. Hold overhead by grasping point X. Let go. Find out if your helicopter turns CLOCKWISE or COUNTERCLOCKWISE. Time how long it takes the helicopter to land. What happens when you fold ROTOR Blades A and B in opposite directions? Make shorter or wider blades? In your Backyard Science Notebook record your results in a chart that looks like the one below. Can you think of a way that you could actually count the number of cycles of your helicopter ROTOR blades in one trial? Color your helicopter. Spin. Look up information on Igor Sikorsky. Tell your friends and family members about his accomplishments and those of Daniel Bernoulli.

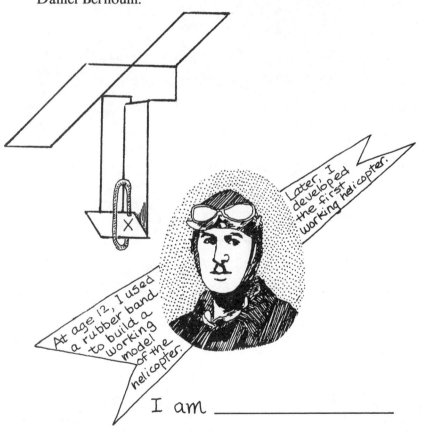

Later, I developed the first working helicopter.

At age 12, I used a rubber band to build a working model of the helicopter.

I am _____

A | B | C

Cut D | | Cut E

Helicopter

Cut F

Blade A | Blade B

Trial Number	Drop Height	Inches	cm	Time in Seconds	Spin: Clockwise/Counterclockwise	Number of Cycles	Other
1							

55

GA1084

Blast into Rocket Cycles

A rocket is an engine or vehicle driven by a rocket engine. It produces a lot of POWER, but also uses a lot of fuel. Before you fly a rocket you will need to know its parts and flight cycle. Using the words below, write the number of the word in the circle that best matches that part of the cycle. Then look up information on Robert Goddard. Write a story about his accomplishments.

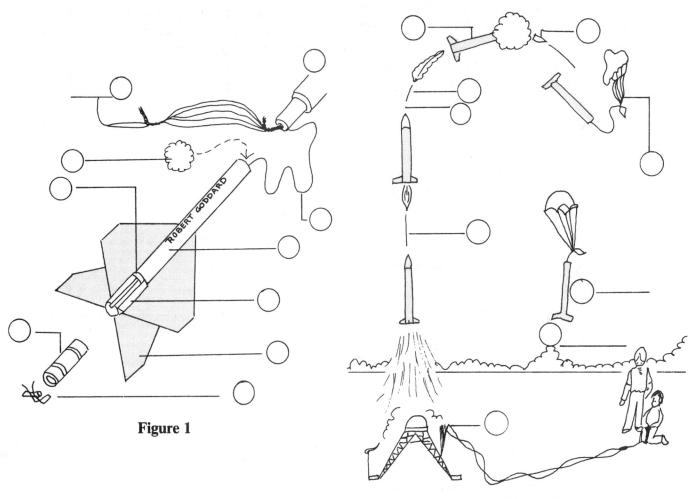

Figure 1

Figure 2

the father of modern rocketry.

I am

I am _____

The Parts of a Model Rocket

1. engine, 2. engine holder, 3. flameproof wadding,
4. folded parachute,
5. nose cone,
6. shock cord,
7. body tube,
8. launch lug, 9. fins,
10. igniter.

The Rocket Cycle

1. lift-off, 2. thrusting flight, 3. burnout, 4. coasting flight,
5. APOGEE (highest point), 6. ejection of recovery system,
7. parachute release,
8. recovery descent,
9. touchdown.

GA1084

Rocket Cycle Blast-Off

Launch a rocket in your backyard. Hang a VERTICAL length of fishline from a tree branch. Tape or glue rocket fins and a straw to a long, narrow balloon. Run fishline through the straw. Attach end of fishline to ground so fishline is tight. Blow up balloon. Release. Observe. Measure the VERTICAL distance traveled by your rocket. Do several trials. Record the results in the chart below. Then soap or wax the fishline. Do more trials. Note changes in distance traveled. Modify your rocket. Measure HORIZONTAL distance traveled by your rocket on clothesline. Record information in chart below. Tell your family members how your experiment shows Newton's Third Law of Motion: for every action, there is an equal and opposite reaction. Then write a letter to Estes Industries, Department 1695, Penrose, CO 81240 requesting further information about rockets.

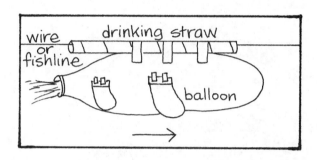

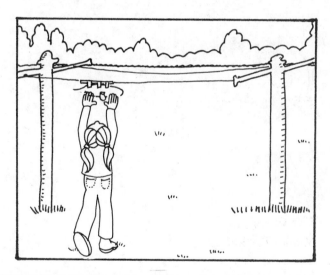

Trial #	Distance traveled (VERTICAL)		Trial #	Distance traveled (HORIZONTAL)	
#1	_____in.	_____cm	#1	_____in.	_____cm
#2	_____in.	_____cm	#2	_____in.	_____cm
#3	_____in.	_____cm	#3	_____in.	_____cm
#4	_____in.	_____cm	#4	_____in.	_____cm
#5	_____in.	_____cm	#5	_____in.	_____cm

GA1084

The Cycles of Wind

Wind is air that moves across the surface of the earth. The cycle of wind begins when the sun heats the ATMOSPHERE unevenly. Air above the hot areas of the earth expands and rises. Air from cooler areas flows in to take the place of the rising hot air. The cycle goes on and on.

Winds are named according to the direction from which they blow. They follow the same cycle but often travel in different directions. The cycle begins at the equator where warm air, heated by the sun, rises and flows away from the equator toward the east. When the air returns to the earth's surface, it moves toward the equator and blows toward the west. Moving surface air produces belts of prevailing winds across the earth. These belts are the Polar Easterlies, Prevailing Westerlies, Horse Latitudes, Trade Winds and Doldrums. Write the correct letter for each belt in the chart. Place in your School Yard Science Notebook for further study.

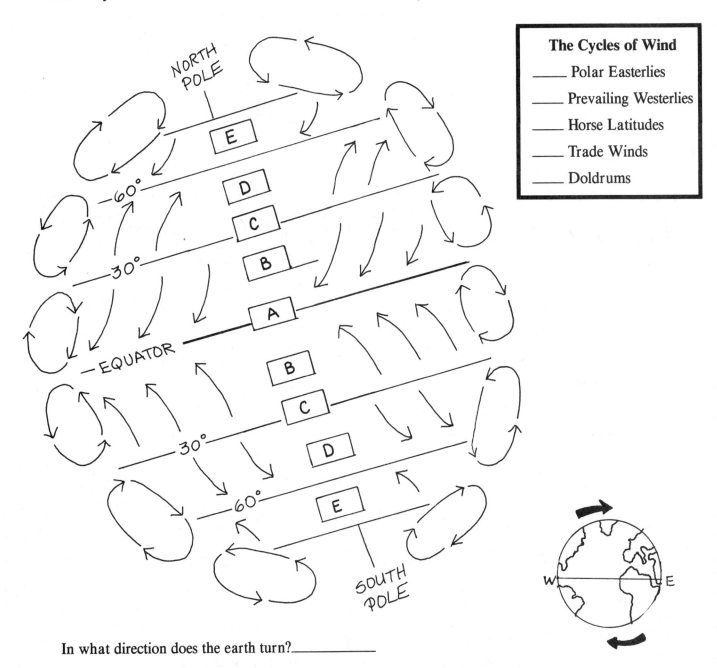

The Cycles of Wind
_____ Polar Easterlies
_____ Prevailing Westerlies
_____ Horse Latitudes
_____ Trade Winds
_____ Doldrums

In what direction does the earth turn?_____

58

GA1084

As the World Turns, Cycles Begin

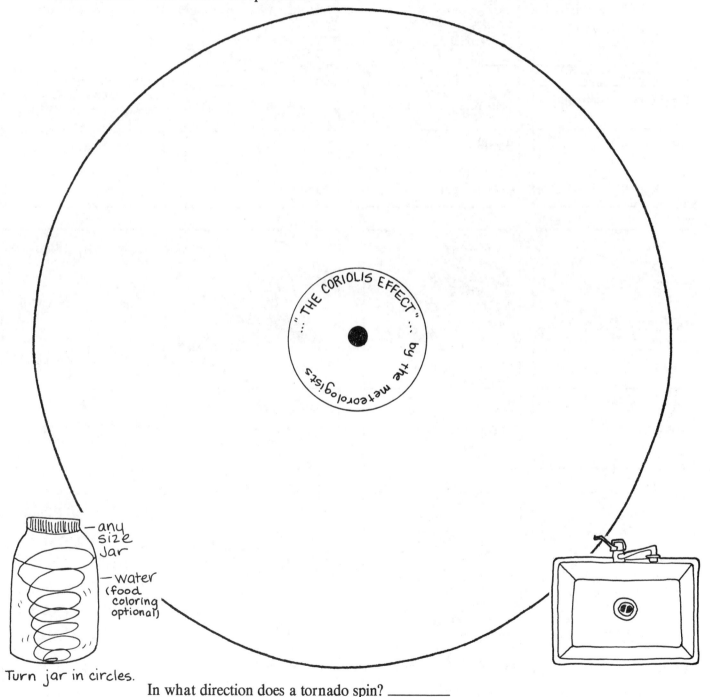

Air moving in cycles is caused by the turning of the earth on its AXIS. As the earth turns, the winds are deflected towards the right in the Northern Hemisphere. This is called the CORIOLIS EFFECT. With help from your parents, cut out a clear piece of plastic the size of the record below. Punch hole in center. Place on record player. Turn on low speed which is like the ROTATION of the earth. With erasable marker, try to draw a straight line across the spinning record. Lift plastic off record player. Look through plastic and note the curved line to the right. Wind in the Northern Hemisphere flows to the right as shown by the line on the plastic. Label the plastic "The Coriolis Effect." Then answer the questions below.

"... THE CORIOLIS EFFECT" ... by the meteorologists

— any size Jar

— water (food coloring optional)

Turn jar in circles.

In what direction does a tornado spin? _____

In what direction does water run down a sink or bathtub? _____

59

GA1084

Beaufort's Cycle: Zero to Ten

BEAUFORT
SCALE

The BEAUFORT SCALE is a wind scale that shows the speed of the wind, the numeral zero for least wind, the numeral twelve for the greatest wind speed. Below are twelve drawings that show the effects of wind. Using an encyclopedia, label each drawing with the appropriate wind speed and BEAUFORT symbol. The first and second cards are done for you. Cut out cards, place in order, and mount on stiff cardboard. Place in your School Yard Science Notebook for further study.

Smoke rises vertically

Beaufort no: 0
Wind speed: less than 1 m.p.h.
Symbol: O

Trees uprooted; buildings severely damaged.

Beaufort no: 10
Wind speed: 55-63 mph. (89-102 km/hr)
Symbol: O-TTTT

Widespread damage

Beaufort no: 11
Wind speed:
Symbol:

Small trees begin to sway; waves on inland waters.

Beaufort no: 5
Wind speed:
Symbol:

Dust and paper raised.

Beaufort no: 4
Wind speed:
Symbol:

Twigs broken off trees.

Beaufort no: 8
Wind speed:
Symbol:

Smoke drifts slightly.

Beaufort no: 1
Wind speed:
Symbol:

Large branches move, umbrellas hard to use.

Beaufort no: 6
Wind speed:
Symbol:

Leaves and twigs in constant motion.

Beaufort no: 3
Wind speed:
Symbol:

Whole trees bend; hard to walk against wind.

Beaufort no: 7
Wind speed:
Symbol:

Buildings damaged.

Beaufort no: 9
Wind speed:
Symbol:

Leaves rustle, vane moved.

Beaufort no: 2
Wind speed:
Symbol:

GA1084

Wind Speed Cycles

An ANEMOMETER is used to measure the speed of the wind. It usually has three or four arms with a cup attached to each arm like this.

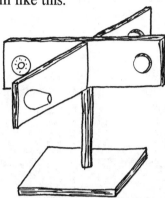

The wind speed is found by counting the number of cycles the ANEMOMETER makes in 30 seconds. Divide that number by 3.5. This gives the approximate wind speed in miles (kilometers) per hour.

Build an ANEMOMETER. Place the bottoms of two 9-inch (23 cm) paper pie plates together. Staple four small paper cups to the pie plates as shown below. Number each cup. Insert pencil through center of pie plates. Use a fan or blow into the first cup to start ANEMOMETER spinning. Count the number of cycles in 30 seconds. Take ANEMOMETER outside on a windy day. Count the cycles for each trial. Record the wind speed. Keep a record of your findings. Place in Backyard Science Notebook for further study.

TIP: Color one cup black. This will help you see and count the number of cycles the anemometer makes in 30 seconds.

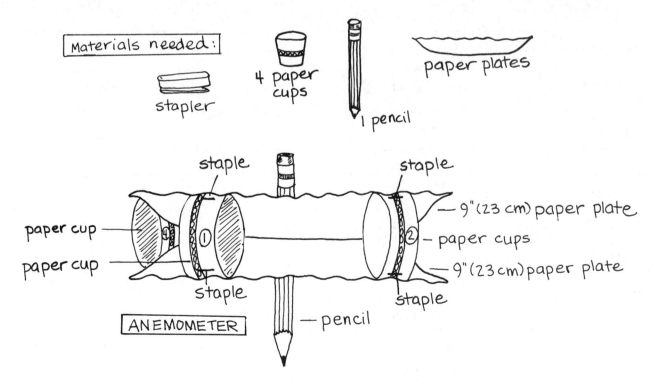

School Yard Rock Cycle Game

The rock cycle begins with hot MAGMA deep inside the earth. MAGMA is made when rocks get so hot they melt. As pressure builds, MAGMA shoots out of the earth and cools to make IGNEOUS rocks. SEDIMENTARY and METAMORPHIC rocks can be made from IGNEOUS rocks. Rocks can be melted down and returned to MAGMA at any stage in the cycle. Play this game with your friends. Use small stones as markers. Roll a die to see who begins the game. Person with the larger number rolls die first. Start at melted rock, MAGMA. Each player rolls die once and in turn moves the number of spaces shown on the die. First person to complete the cycle and return to melted rock, MAGMA, wins the game.

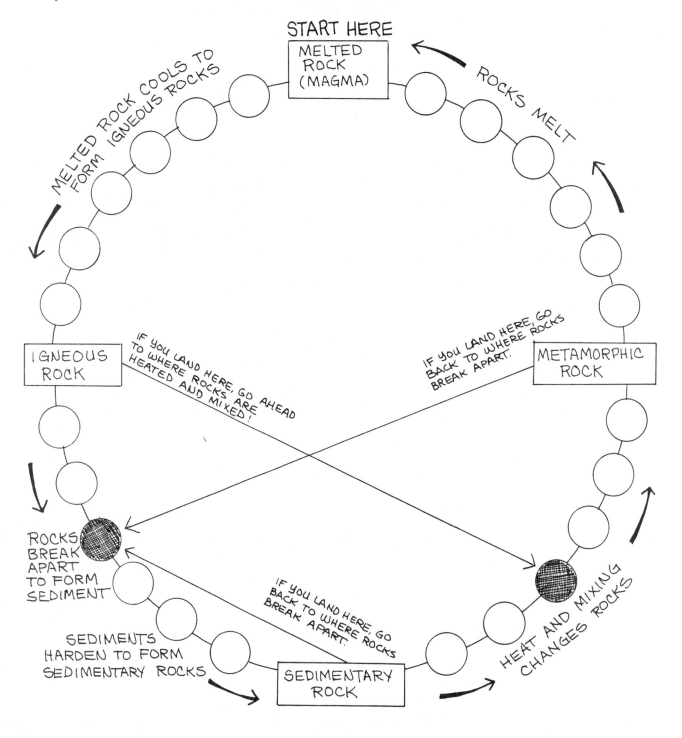

GA1084

Backyard Rock Cycle

Go outside and find five small but different rocks. Using a piece of tape, label the rocks A, B, C, D and E. Make a record of where and when each rock was found. Carefully clean each rock. Do MOHS' tests on each rock. Write results in the charts below. On cardboard, tape your rocks in order by hardness using MOHS' scale as your guide. Learn this device to help you remember the order of rocks in MOHS' scale: The Girls Can Flirt And Feel Queer, Then Comes Diamonds. Then classify the twelve rocks below as igneous, sedimentary or metamorphic.

MY ROCK CHART

Rock	Color wet	dry	SHADE	WEIGHT	LAYERS	TEXTURE rough smooth	WRITES yes no	SHINY or DULL	CRYSTALS	VINEGAR ADDED	MOHS' RATING	SPECIFIC GRAVITY	OTHER
A													
B													
C													
D													
E													

MOHS' SCALE CHART

ROCK	Finger-nail	Penny	Nail	Knife	Glass	Tile	Color	Other
A								
B								
C								
D								
E								

*MOHS' SCALE OF RELATIVE HARDNESS

MATERIAL	WHAT IT WILL DO	Rating
TALC	so soft it's used for talcum powder	1
GYPSUM	a fingernail will scratch it	2
CALCITE	a copper penny will scratch it	3
FLUORITE	a steel knife will scratch it	4
APATITE	a knife scratches if you press hard	5
FELDSPAR	will scratch a knife blade	6
QUARTZ	will scratch glass (& all previous)	7
TOPAZ	will scratch quartz (& all previous)	8
CORUNDUM	will scratch all except a diamond	9
DIAMOND	will scratch everything	10

Write the names of these twelve rocks in the proper spaces below: Granite, Slate, Conglomerate, Basalt, Schist, Marble, Quartzite, Sandstone, Obsidian, Shale, Diorite, Limestone.

IGNEOUS	SEDIMENTARY	METAMORPHIC
1. _____	1. _____	1. _____
2. _____	2. _____	2. _____
3. _____	3. _____	3. _____
4. _____	4. _____	4. _____

GA1084

The Nutrient Cycle

Plants, animals and small microscopic creatures live in the soil made up of broken down rocks. They are called DECOMPOSERS because they break down dead plants and animals. NUTRIENTS from these materials are returned to the soil where plants can once again use these to grow. Below are pictures that show the stages of a nutrient cycle. Cut out the pictures. Glue pictures, in order, to a piece of cardboard. Find out the role that a COMPOST plays in a garden. Then make a tape of the following ode. Play tape to the class.

TIP: It takes 500 years to make one inch of soil from broken down rocks.

The End: An Ode to the Recyclers

We may not always like them or their odors. Many forms cause diseases. Without *bacteria* and *fungi*, however, all life on this planet would cease. Only *bacteria*, *fungi* and a few protozoans have the ENZYMES to break down *cellulose* (wood) and recycle its components to the earth and air. They are the final decomposers of all plant and animal matter. Without them, there would be no decay, no soil and thus *NO LIFE*.

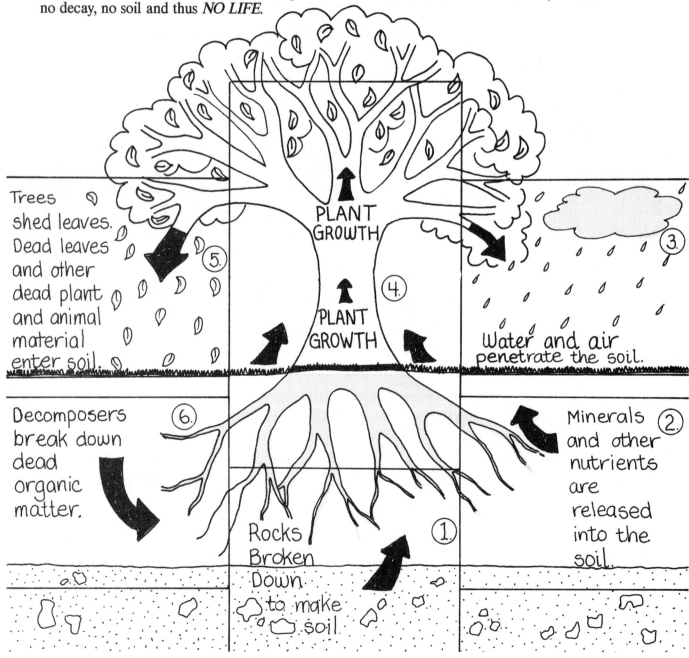

Trees shed leaves. Dead leaves and other dead plant and animal material enter soil. ⑤

PLANT GROWTH

③

PLANT GROWTH ④

Water and air penetrate the soil.

Decomposers break down dead organic matter. ⑥

Rocks Broken Down to make soil ①

Minerals ② and other nutrients are released into the soil.

64

GA1084

Nutrient Cycle in the Soil

Go outside and collect a spoonful of SOIL from each of four areas in your backyard. Place a spoonful of SOIL in each circle below. With a hand lens, examine each soil sample. On a piece of paper, make a list of plants and animals found in each SOIL sample. Tell your family members about the role that these ORGANISMS play in the nutrient cycle.

GA1084

Water: the Cycle of Life

On earth, water travels in cycles as it changes from a solid to a liquid to a gas and back again to a liquid and a solid. In the WATER CYCLE, water goes through three stages: EVAPORATION, CONDENSATION and PRECIPITATION. On the cards below, write the name of each stage.

Place this sheet in a clear plastic bag. Using an eyedropper, place a drop of water on 1. Tilt page so drop travels between 1-2-3-4-1. This shows how water travels through three stages in the WATER CYCLE. Name each stage. Place in your School Yard Science Notebook for further study.

GA1084

Water Cycle in the Kitchen

Below is a picture of how you can observe the water cycle in your home. With help from your parents, place cookie sheet with ice cubes over heated kettle on stove. Observe the evaporation of water from the kettle as it rises and strikes the underside of the cold cookie sheet. Note condensation on underside. With container in hand, catch water droplets as they fall in the form of precipitation from the cookie sheet. Count the drops. Remove cookie sheet with ice cubes. Observe what happens to STEAM coming from kettle. Compare to condensation of WATER VAPOR on a hot summer day on the underside of a sheet of clear plastic placed over grass or water on the sides of a cold jar of lemonade. Tell your family members the three stages in the water cycle: evaporation, condensation and precipitation. In your notebook, define the words STEAM and WATER VAPOR. Use the glossary for your definitions. Then study how the water cycle is related to the weather.

GA1084

Food Cycle

PLANTS
MEAT

We need food to live. Below are twelve cards that show how PLANTS are grown and eaten by animals who give us MEAT to eat. Cut out the cards below. Arrange pictures in order. Then glue to a piece of cardboard. Observe the order of the pictures carefully. Choose one food that you ate in school today. In your School Yard Science Notebook, draw a set of pictures that shows what happened to the food before you ate it for lunch today.

Cow eats corn.

Farmer picks corn.

Waste materials fertilize the soil.

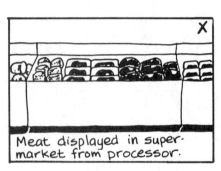

Meat displayed in super-market from processor.

Cows go to stockyard slaughterhouse.

Meat cooks in oven.

Farmer cultivates small corn plants.

People go to super-market to purchase meat.

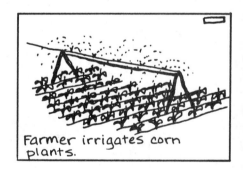

Farmer irrigates corn plants.

People eat meat.

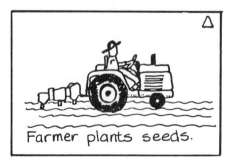

Farmer plants seeds.

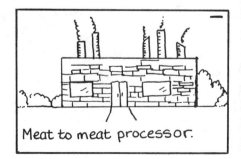

Meat to meat processor.

GA1084

Plant Food Cycle:
Goober's More Pea Than Nut

People grow plants for food to eat. One such plant is a peanut which is not really a NUT but rather a kind of pea. The peanut is a LEGUME. It's unusual because its PODS, which contain seeds, grow underground. The peanut plant has an interesting cycle. Its flowers grow at dawn, wilt and fall to the ground at noon. A stem forms, pushes into the soil and its tip grows into a peanut POD. We eat some of the seeds in the POD; others grow into new peanut plants. The cycle continues. Below is a picture of a peanut plant. Obtain some dry roasted and salted-in-the-shell peanuts. Write the answers to the questions below on the matching peanuts. Using an encyclopedia, read about the works of George Washington Carver while you eat your peanuts.

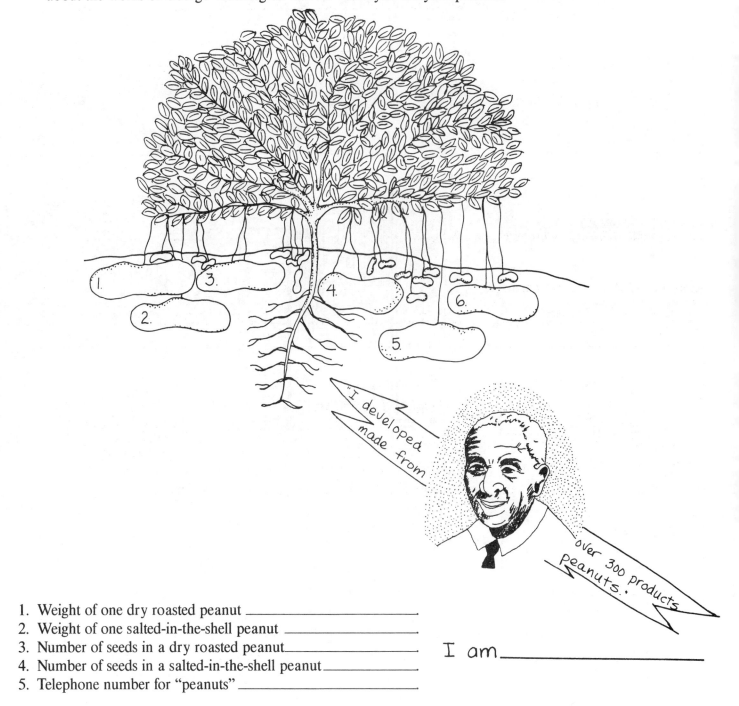

"I developed made from over 300 products Peanuts."

1. Weight of one dry roasted peanut _____
2. Weight of one salted-in-the-shell peanut _____
3. Number of seeds in a dry roasted peanut_____
4. Number of seeds in a salted-in-the-shell peanut_____
5. Telephone number for "peanuts" _____

I am _____

GA1084

Space Recycle

To RECYCLE means to pass again through a cycle of change. In space, many things are used over and over again. Below is a picture of a space shuttle. Cut out the recycling symbols below. Tape or glue these symbols on the parts of the space shuttle that will be retrieved and used again once the space shuttle is in orbit. Find out at what point in the launch these objects fall from the shuttle to be retrieved and reused. Then name and color your shuttle.

TIP: Write a letter requesting information on how you can become involved in the space program to: Space Science Student Involvement Program, National Science Teachers Association, 1742 Connecticut Avenue, N.W., Washington, D.C. 20009

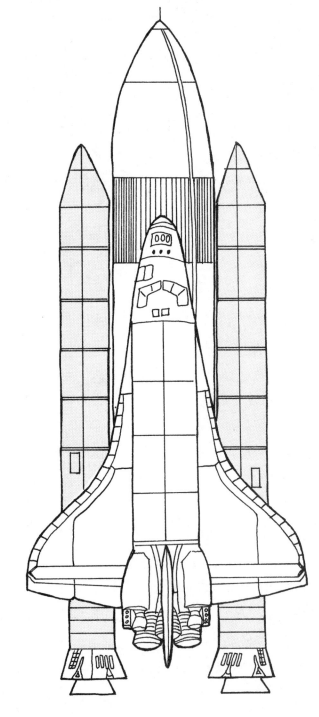

GA1084

School Yard(S)-Backyard(B)
Biological Science Cycles

Here are some pictures of activities that you and your youngsters will encounter in this section.

GA1084

Life Cycle of a Mealworm

A mealworm is a creature that often lives in cereals and cereal products. It feeds on grain or flour and is often found in mills or granaries. The mealworm has a life cycle of four stages as shown on the cards below. Write the correct name for each stage on each card. Cut out cards. Rearrange the cards in order to show the life cycle of a mealworm. Mount cards, in order, on a stiff piece of cardboard. Carefully study the cards. How many legs does a mealworm have? Try to find out how many friends would be needed to walk like a mealworm. Then do it. After walking, have each of your friends be a part of the cycle of a mealworm. Present to the class for all to see.

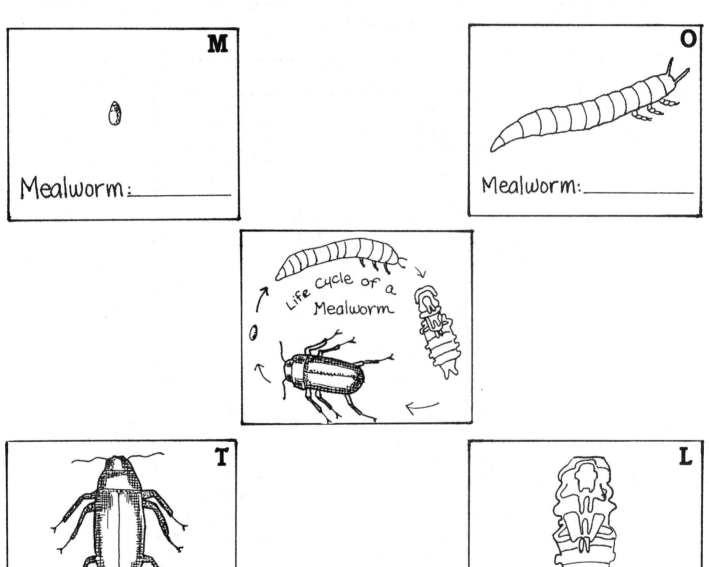

M Mealworm:_____

O Mealworm:_____

Life Cycle of a Mealworm

T Mealworm:_____

L Mealworm:_____

Words to Choose from: Adult, Egg, Larva, Pupa

GA1084

Can a Mealworm Smell?

BEHAVIOR

To find out whether your mealworm can smell, you will need a shoe box lid and some scratch and sniff stickers. If mealworms cannot be obtained from a mill or granary, they can be purchased rather inexpensively at a pet shop. Write an "X" in the center of underside of a shoe box lid. Label this "start zone." Stick four different smell stickers, one in each corner of the box. Place mealworm in "start zone." Observe direction in which the mealworm travels to its favorite smell sticker. Note its BEHAVIOR. Record your findings in the chart below. Do at least fifty trials. The smell chosen the greatest number of times by your mealworm is its favorite smell.

TIP: When finished, place your mealworm in a plastic container. Add bran or cereal for food and a small piece of apple for water. Observe its life cycle.

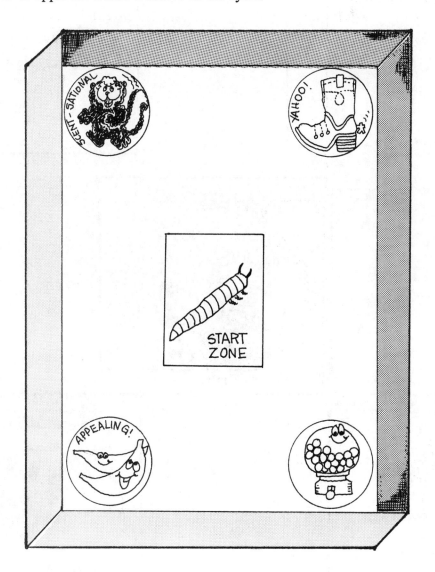

Trial #	Sticker 1	Sticker 2	Sticker 3	Sticker 4	My mealworm's favorite smell is:
1					
2					
3					

GA1084

Life Cycle of a Monarch Butterfly

Butterflies are interesting insects to observe because they are always changing their appearance. Every butterfly goes through four different stages in its life cycle. During each stage the butterfly changes its looks. The process of growing through these stages is called METAMORPHOSIS. On the cards below, write the name for each stage. Cut out each card. Mount cards, in order, on a stiff piece of cardboard. If correct, you will learn the Monarch's favorite plant. Observe cards carefully. Then make a butterfly using colored paper or cellophane.

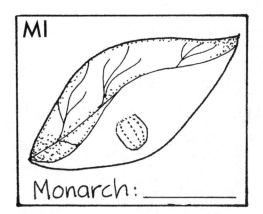

MI

Monarch: _____

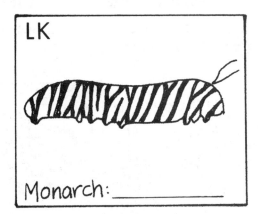

LK

Monarch: _____

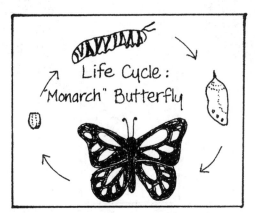

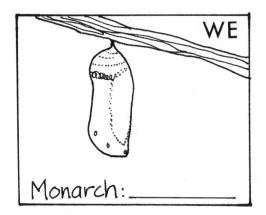

WE

Monarch: _____

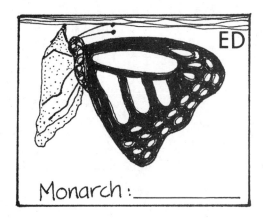

ED

Monarch: _____

Words to Choose from: Egg, Larva (caterpillar), Pupa (chrysalis), Adult

74

GA1084

Observe the Life Cycle of a Butterfly

Below are pictures of two famous butterflies. Write their names on the cards. In the spring find a monarch caterpillar on a milkweed or dogbane plant. (The swallowtail caterpillar is found on carrot tops, parsley, dill or fennel plants.) Make a home for your CATERPILLAR using a large box or plastic container. Cut out windows. Cover with netting. Put CATERPILLAR in the container. Add food which is often found where you found the caterpillar. Observe your caterpillar closely. Keep a record of its changes.

A

My name: _____

B

My name: _____

C

My name: _____

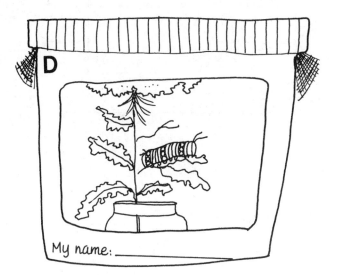

D

My name: _____

GA1084

Life Cycle of a Cecropia Moth

Moths are different from butterflies in that moths are NOCTURNAL, butterflies DIURNAL. Compare moths to butterflies below. Write "M" in the blank if the feature is that of a moth, a "B" for butterfly. On the large cards below, write the name of each stage. Cut out each card. Mount cards, in order, on stiff cardboard. Place in your School Yard Science Notebook for further study.

 CLUBBED ANTENNA _____   WINGS OVER BACK AT REST _____   FEATHERED ANTENNA _____   WINGS DOWN OR AT SIDE AT REST _____

 NOCTURNAL _____   STOCKY BODY _____   DIURNAL _____   NARROW PINCHED BODY _____

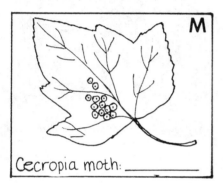

Cecropia moth: _____ **M**

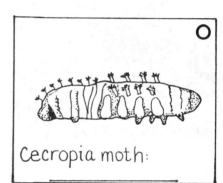

Cecropia moth: _____ **O**

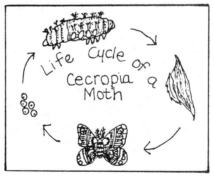

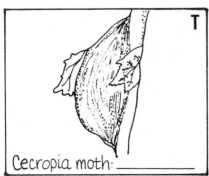

Cecropia moth: _____ **T**

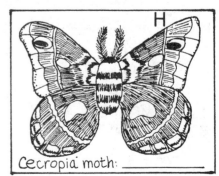

Cecropia moth: _____ **H**

Words to Choose from: Eggs, Larva, Pupa (cocoon), Adult

76

GA1084

Observe the Life Cycle
of a Cecropia Moth

You can observe the life cycle of a cecropia moth (found in Midwest to East Coast in U.S.) or its relative the polyphemus moth found throughout the U.S. and Canada. Search for the cecropia caterpillar on trees that it feeds upon such as green pussy willow leaves, purple plum leaves, green lilac leaves and green wild cherry leaves. The polyphemus caterpillars feed on a variety of trees such as maple, birch, hickory and oak. Below are pictures of the cecropia moth egg and caterpillar. In the spring, find a cecropia caterpillar. Make a home for your caterpillar. Cut windows in a large plastic container. Cover with netting. Include leaves for food. Observe caterpillar closely. Note its color and **TUBERCLES.** Fill in the blanks below. Keep this record in your Backyard Science Notebook. Share with your family members.

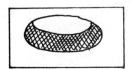

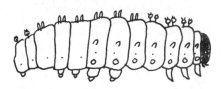

Cecropia Moth Egg

Cecropia Moth Caterpillar

1. Color of cecropia moth egg _____

2. Shape of cecropia moth egg _____

3. Color of cecropia moth caterpillar _____

4. Color of four front **TUBERCLES** _____

5. Color and feel of very young cecropia moth caterpillar _____

6. Season(s) during which this moth's silken cocoon can be found hanging

   from bare tree branches _____

7. My special name for cecropia moth caterpillar _____

8. Four stages in the life cycle of a cecropia moth (1) _____,

   (2) _____, (3) _____, (4) _____

—netting

Life Cycle of a Mosquito

Mosquitoes are popular insects and have an interesting life cycle. At each stage in a mosquito's life, shown on the cards below, the mosquito changes its looks completely and lives a different kind of lifestyle. Cut out each card. Print the name of the stage on each card. Rearrange in order to show the life cycle of a mosquito. Mount cards, in order, on a stiff piece of cardboard. Place in your School Yard Science Notebook for further study.

TIP: A mosquito has a hard life. Ten to twenty percent of all hatched mosquitoes die shortly after birth. In the wild, mosquitoes live less than two months.

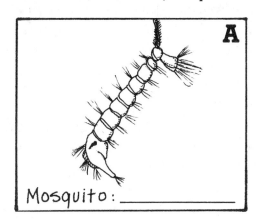

Mosquito: _____ A

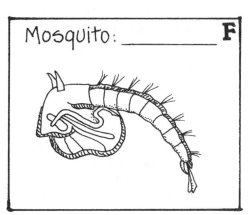

Mosquito: _____ F

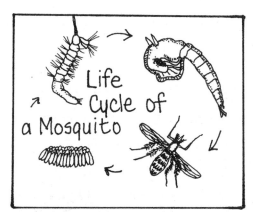

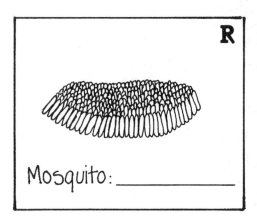

Mosquito: _____ R

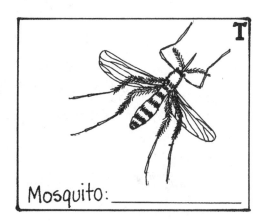

Mosquito: _____ T

Words to choose from: Egg Raft, Larva (wriggler), Pupa (tumbler), Adult

78

GA1084

Mosquito Watch

The life cycle of a male mosquito lasts about twenty days, the female about thirty days or more. During their life cycle, some mosquitoes carry germs that cause serious diseases such as yellow fever and malaria. Other mosquitoes do not spread diseases but rather "bite" people. Only females "bite" people. They need the victim's blood to develop eggs inside their bodies.

People control mosquitoes by destroying the wet places in which they grow with INSECTICIDES, or with thin layers of oil. You can do the same. In the spring or summer, fill three small plastic trays with water. In one container add a thin layer of oil; in another add a thin spray of insect repellant; third, leave open water. Using a bright light, attract a SWARM of mosquitoes. Observe what happens as the mosquitoes approach each of the containers. To which container are the greatest number of mosquitoes attracted? Record your results in your Backyard Science Notebook. Then study the words of Walter Reed and how he found out that yellow fever called "yellow jack" was caused by a virus carried from one person to another by a female mosquito. In what city is Walter Reed Army Medical Center located? Fill in the blanks below.

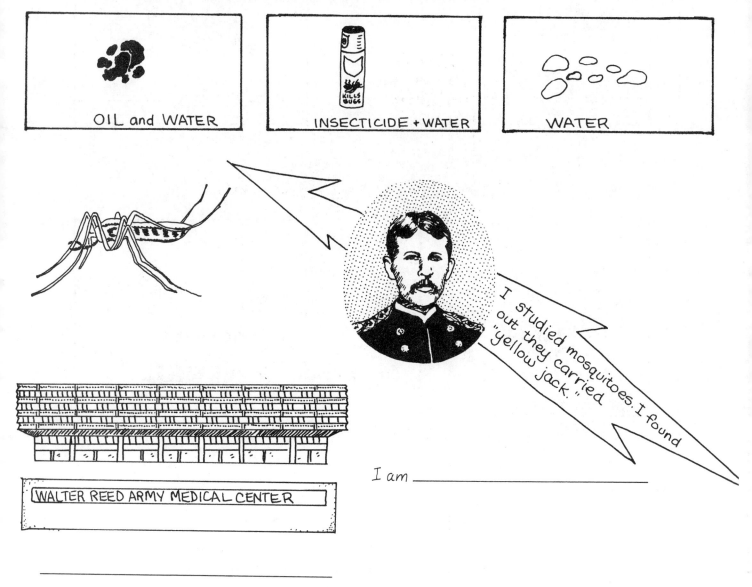

OIL and WATER

INSECTICIDE + WATER

WATER

I studied mosquitoes. I found out they carried "yellow jack."

I am _____

WALTER REED ARMY MEDICAL CENTER

_____

City: Walter Reed Army Medical Center

GA1084

Life Cycle of a Grasshopper

Some insects go through incomplete metamorphosis which means they do not go through larval and pupal stages. One such insect is the grasshopper. When the young hopper hatches, it is called a NYMPH. It looks like a little adult without wings. As it grows, the hopper MOLTS. This means that it splits its skin and crawls out. Grasshoppers do this six times before they become an adult with wings. On the cards below, write the name of each stage in the life cycle of a grasshopper. Cut out each card. Mount cards, in order, on stiff cardboard. Color each stage in a grasshopper's life cycle. Place in your School Yard Science Notebook for further study.

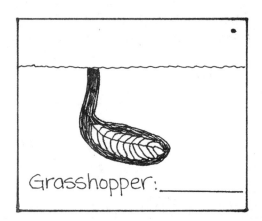

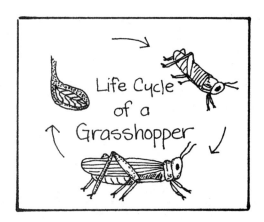

Words to Choose from: Egg, Nymph, Adult

GA1084

Grasshopper Hop

Grasshoppers are some of the world's greatest leapers. They are found in the backyard, marshes, fields, deserts and forests. Go outside in the summer. Capture a grasshopper. Observe its strong, tiny muscles in its back legs. These help the grasshopper leap. Grasshoppers can sometimes jump a distance twenty-five times their *length* while humans can jump forward only three times their *height*. Measure the length of your grasshopper. Record this length and that of your height in the charts below. Place grasshopper on a starting line. Measure the distance jumped. Record. Now it's your turn. Place toes on line. Jump forward. Measure distance jumped. Record. Find out the number of times its length the grasshopper can jump. Do the same for yourself. Did you or the grasshopper win?

TIP: After various trials, release your tired grasshopper into its natural HABITAT. NOTE: If a grasshopper cannot be found, use a cricket or bounce a tennis ball the approximate distance that a grasshopper can jump from the starting line.

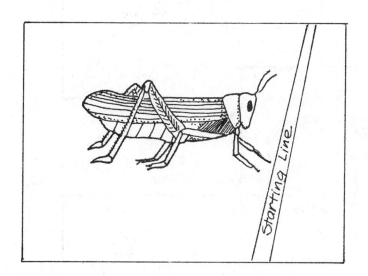

My Grasshopper / Me

Trial #	Length	Distance Jumped	# of Times Length	Trial #	Height	Distance Jumped	# of Times Height
1				1			
2				2			
3				3			

GA1084

Life Cycle of a Ladybird Beetle

Ladybird beetles are one of many helpful insects. As PREDATORS, they feed on harmful insects such as aphids, potato beetles and maple scale. On the cards below, write the name of each stage in the life cycle of a ladybird beetle. Cut out each card. Mount cards, in order, on stiff cardboard. Color your ladybird beetle. Then place the cards in your School Yard Science Notebook for further study.

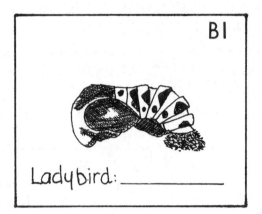

BI

Ladybird: _____

DY

Ladybird: _____

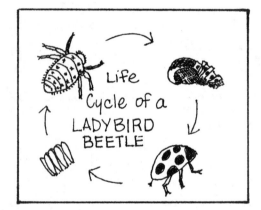

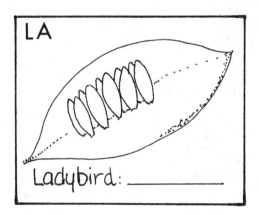

LA

Ladybird: _____

RD

Ladybird: _____

Words to Choose from: Egg, Larva, Pupa, Adult

GA1084

Ladybird Launch

PREY

Ladybird larvae and ladybird beetle adults eat many harmful insects. Use these to grow healthier food in your garden. Go outside. List at least two common insect pests found in your backyard that a ladybird beetle could PREY upon. Write their names on Card #1. Describe the problem caused by these insects on Card #2. Look up the name, address and telephone number of your nearest Cooperative Extension Service. Record this information on Card #3. Then call the Cooperative Extension Service (local government) for information on the care, purchase and use of ladybird beetles to control harmful insects. Fill in Card #4 below. Then release your ladybird beetles to control the insect pests found in your backyard.

Two Insect Pests Card #1	Pest Problem Card #2
1.	1.
2.	2.

| My Cooperative Extension   Card #3
 Service Calling Card

 Name _____

 Address _____
 _____

 Phone_____ | Ladybird Beetle Information   Card #4

 Care of Ladybird Beetles

 Cost:

 Benefits:

 Release Date: |

GA1084

Life Cycle of a Frog

Frogs are animals called AMPHIBIANS. Most AMPHIBIANS spend part of their lives both in the water and on land. They are COLD-BLOODED which means that their body temperature is about the same as the surrounding air or water temperature. Below are pictures that show the four stages in the life cycle of a frog. Name each stage. Cut out the pictures. Glue pictures, in order, to a piece of cardboard. Study the cards carefully. Color each. Place in your School Yard Science Notebook for further study. Then play leap frog with four friends, each of whom is a different frog stage. You must leap over each individual stage (friend) to become an adult frog.

E

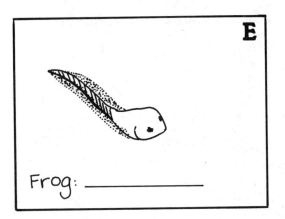

Frog: _____

A

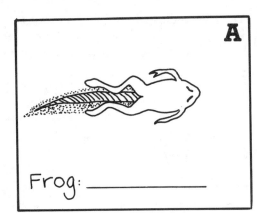

Frog: _____

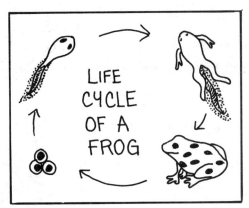

L

Frog: _____

P

Frog: _____

Words to Choose from: Eggs, Tadpole Without Legs, Tadpole with Legs, Adult

GA1084

Frog Cuts

Frogs help people because they eat insect pests, provide us with food and allow students to dissect them to learn about ANATOMY. Below are pictures of a frog's organs. Also shown is a blank picture of a frog whose belly has been cut open. Cut out each organ below starting with number one, kidneys. Tape tip of organ to correct location on frog. Glue remaining organs by the tips to correct locations. These can be easily lifted to expose the organ below. Find out and record in your notebook what each organ does to keep the frog alive.

TIP: Organs 3-6 may be glued on top of organs 1 and 2 at point X for easy lift to view.

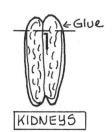

← Glue here

HEART,
LIVER,
GALL BLADDER

← Glue here

LUNGS

← Glue

KIDNEYS

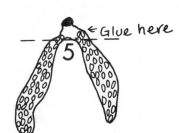

← Glue here

← Glue here

STOMACH,
INTESTINES

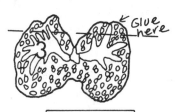

Glue here

OVARIES

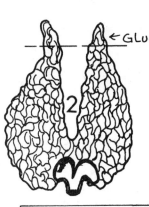

OVIDUCTS (Female)

85

GA1084

Life Cycle of a Tree

Some trees live over 4000 years. All trees begin as tiny seeds. A single tree grows and produces many seeds during its lifetime. These trees are called PERENNIALS because they live through many seasons. Most trees become DORMANT in winter, but their twigs, branches, stems, trunk and roots are alive and continue to grow. Below is a picture of an oak tree. Label its parts. Cut out the cards in its life cycle. Mount cards, in order, on stiff cardboard. Study the tree's life cycle from seed to advanced age.

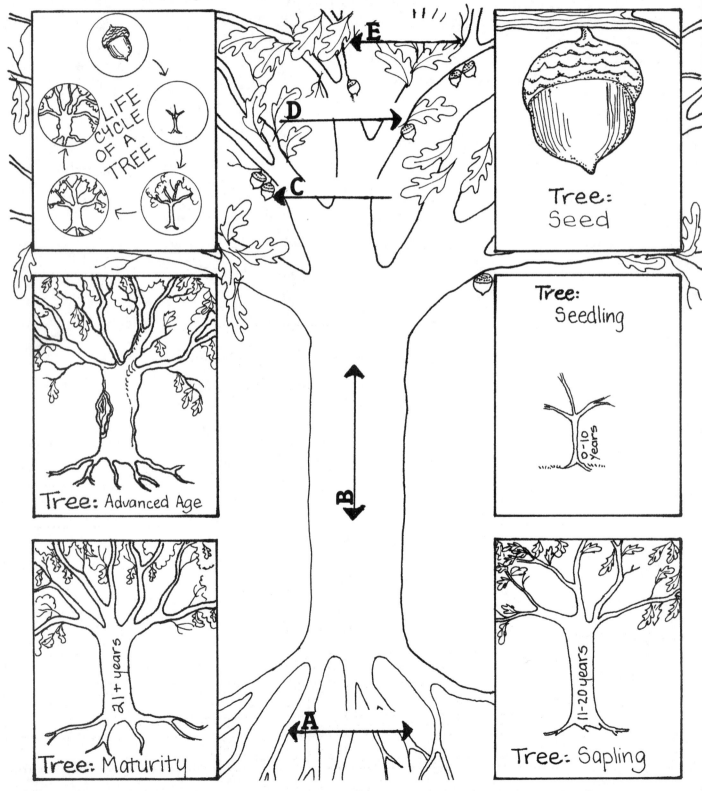

86

Log Lore

You can identify the age of a tree and some factors that influenced its growth by counting its annual growth RINGS. Go outside. Find a log like one used for firewood. It will look like this from the end.

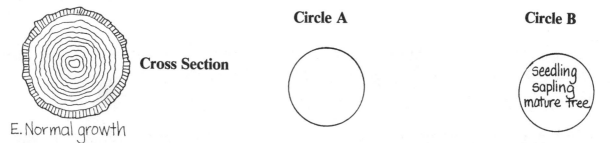

Circle A

Circle B

Cross Section

seedling
sapling
mature tree

E. Normal growth

Push a pin into the center of the log, the birthday of the tree. Count the number of rings outward to learn the age of the tree, one ring per year. Record that number in Circle A above. In Circle B, circle the word that tells whether the tree was a SEEDLING, SAPLING, or mature tree. See page 86 for clues.

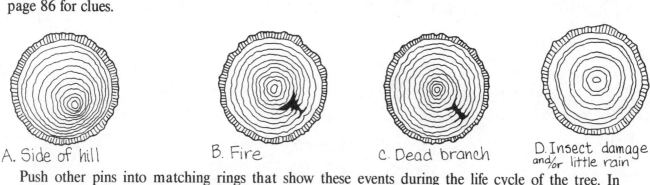

A. Side of hill   B. Fire   C. Dead branch   D. Insect damage and/or little rain

Push other pins into matching rings that show these events during the life cycle of the tree. In the blanks below, record the *first* year in which that event began to occur.

TIP: Study pictures A, B, C, D above to answer questions 3-7 below. Place letter in the correct blank.

General Information:	Record	Clues: Look for and Do This
1. Year in which the *tree* was born		center of log
2. Year in which *I* was born		count your age out from center of log
3. Year(s) of little rain		rings close together in groups
4. Year(s) in which tree grew on a side of a hill		rings toward one side of tree
5. Year(s) in which a forest fire scarred the tree		charred wood, carbon in rings
6. Year in which a dead branch fell off the tree		scar across several rings
7. Year in which insects damaged the tree		close rings followed by wide apart rings

GA1084

Life Cycle of an Apple Tree

Apple trees are tall; some grow to be 40 feet (12 meters) tall and live 40-100 years. There are four stages in the life cycle of an apple tree. These stages are repeated over and over again. To grow an apple tree, one cuts BUDS from a healthy tree and grafts the BUDS to a ROOTSTOCK (root and stem) of a tree. This tree will then bear apples of the same kind of the tree from which the BUDS came. Below are pictures of the life cycle of a tree. Cut out the pictures, place in order and glue to red construction paper. In the space on each picture, write the correct name (dormant, BLOSSOM, fruit set, ripe fruit) for that stage. When finished, place your cards in your School Yard Science Notebook for further study. Then have an apple for lunch today.

TIP: Hard, freshly picked apples can be stored in a cold, humid place up to eight months.

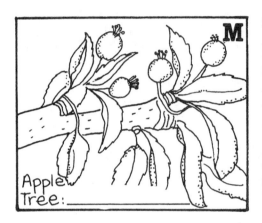

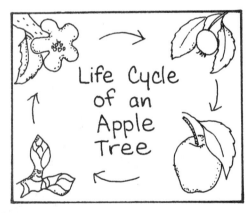

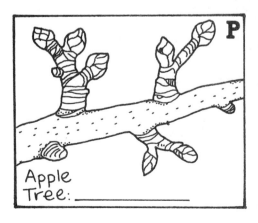

GA1084

Apple Pome

Apple trees grow best in a place that has cold winters. The fruit from an apple tree does not grow in winter, but an apple tree needs this DORMANT season to live. In late spring, white blossoms open. These are POLLINATED by insects such as bees. Seeds begin to grow in the OVARY of the POLLINATED flower. The OVARY and other parts of the flower grow into a fruit in 60-200 days. The apple grows into a POME because it is a fruit with a fleshy outer layer and a paperlike core. A POME also has more than one seed in its core. To find out how many, obtain two apples. Cut one apple in half *lengthwise*. Observe its outer layer and paperlike core. Observe the stem. Count the number of seeds. Draw a picture of this cut-apart apple in Apple A below. Cut the second apple in half *crosswise*. Observe the pattern made by the seeds. Count the seeds. Draw a picture of this cut-apart apple in Apple B below. What shape did you find in the apple? Compare both apples. How are they the same? Different? Dry the seeds. Conclude your study by eating the apple and planting one of the seeds. Then read about the experiences of Johnny Appleseed in an encyclopedia.

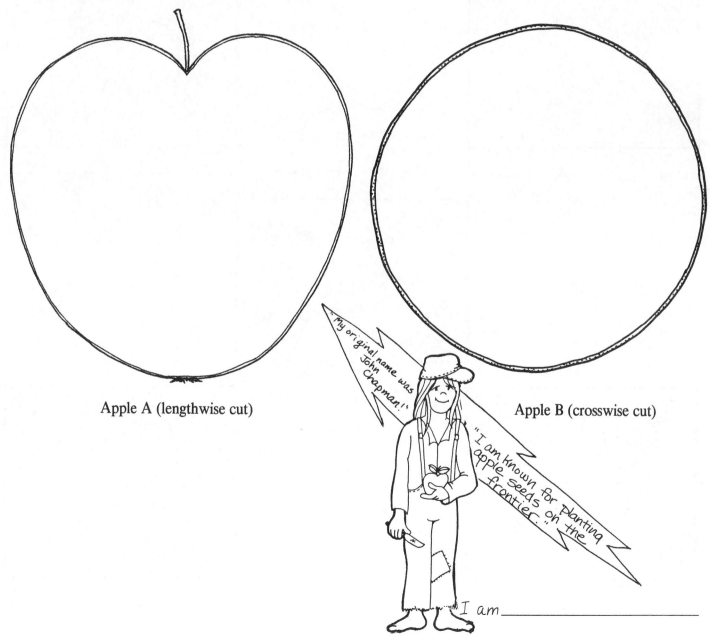

Apple A (lengthwise cut)

Apple B (crosswise cut)

"My original name was John Chapman!"

"I am known for planting apple seeds on the frontier."

I am _____

GA1084

From Cells to Systems

All living things are made up of CELLS. A CELL is alive. It takes in food. It gets rid of wastes. It grows and usually creates two more cells. In time, the cell dies.

As cells die, new cells are born to replace the dead ones. White blood cells live about 12 days, red blood cells 120 days, liver cells 540 days and nerve cells 100 years. The cycle goes on and on. There are different kinds of cells such as blood cells, skin cells, muscle cells and nerve cells. Living cells get together to form TISSUES which get together to form ORGANS and organs make up a SYSTEM. Below are pictures that show these groups of CELLS. Cut out and name each. Glue pictures, in order, to a piece of cardboard. Place in your School Yard Science Notebook for further study.

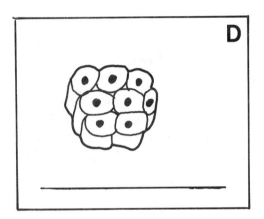

D

_____

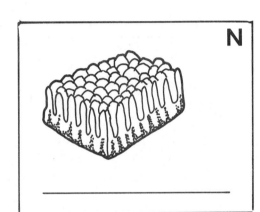

N

_____

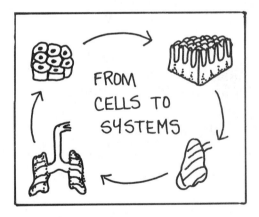

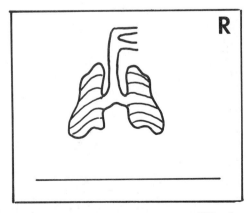

R

_____

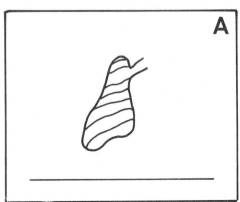

A

_____

Words to Choose from: Organ, Cells, System, Tissue

90

GA1084

Life Cycle of a Cell

YOLK

All plants and animals are made up of cells. You are made up of millions of cells. Each cell goes through a life cycle from birth until death. Dead cells from organs inside your body are passed out of the body. To replace these cells, billions of cells are made each day. The cycle goes on and on. You can observe dead cells being shed from your body. Peel a tiny, loose piece of skin from your body. Tape it inside Box A. Observe the skin. You won't be able to see a single

Box A

Box B

skin cell because it is too small. However, you can see a very large cell—the YOLK of a bird's egg. With help from your parents, crack a chicken egg into a frying pan. Carefully observe the yellow YOLK, one of the largest cells known. Cut out a circle of paper about the size of the YOLK. Glue this in Box B. Color the paper YOLK. Compare it to the size of the real YOLK. Fry, then eat your egg. Enjoy a laugh. "The YOLK'S on you," said a fifth grade boy. He added, "Which came first, the egg or chicken?"

CHICKEN

EGG

GA1084

Monthly Cycle of Menstruation

Between the ages of 9 and 16, boys and girls experience many changes in their bodies. These changes occur at PUBERTY which is when a boy becomes capable of fatherhood; a girl, motherhood. As girls approach womanhood, they begin to experience menstruation. At this time, the lining of a special organ called the UTERUS begins to shed. This happens once per month for a "PERIOD" of several days. Thus, menstruation is often called a girl's PERIOD. Below are four information and four picture cards. Cut out and match the information cards to the picture cards. Glue the cards, in order, to construction paper. Identify the symbols on the cards. Place in your School Yard Science Notebook for further study.

♀

A special lining of blood and tissue grows in the uterus to prepare a home for the egg to grow into a baby, if it is fertilized (united with a sperm).

xy

About two weeks before a girl gets her "period," one egg cell matures, leaves the ovary, enters the fallopian tube and travels toward the UTERUS. Pregnancy can occur at this time, but this can vary from month to month.

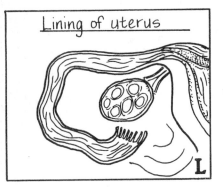

Lining of uterus

L

Ovulation

O

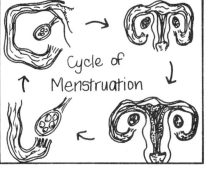

Cycle of Menstruation

xx

As a girl begins to reach PUBERTY, thousands of egg cells develop in her ovaries inside her body.

♂

If the egg is not fertilized, the special lining is no longer needed so it and the broken up egg cell flow out of the girl's body. This flow is called "the PERIOD."

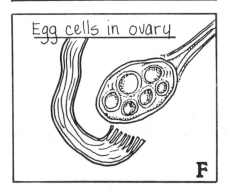

Egg cells in ovary

F

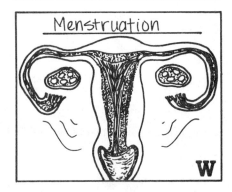

Menstruation

W

GA1084

Old Wives' Tales and the Cycle of Menstruation

Until this century, scientists and doctors knew very little about MENSTRUATION. Because of this, people told many strange stories. With more information, these old wives' tales were proven false. Most girls and women can actually participate in regular activities during MENSTRUATION. To understand this further, it is important for a girl to talk with someone close to her. That person may be her mother, sister or a relative. Ask about the physical and emotional changes related to MENSTRUATION. Record that information in your private diary below.

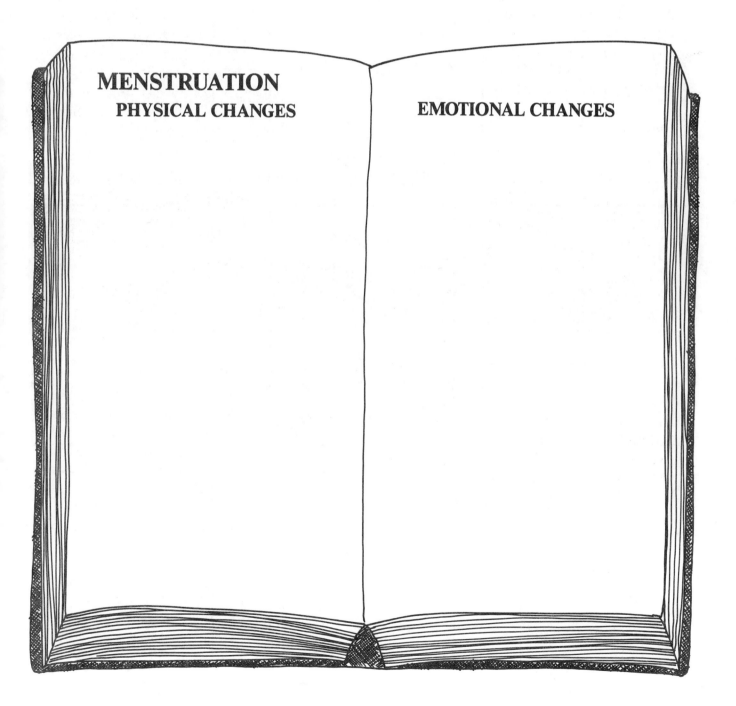

MENSTRUATION
PHYSICAL CHANGES

EMOTIONAL CHANGES

GA1084

Conception to Birth Cycle

Before youngsters are born, they float around in a sac filled with fluid inside their mothers. While they grow, they go through various stages. Here are nine cards that show these stages. Cut apart the cards. On each card write the day or week that matches that stage of growth. Your choices are Day 1, Day 7, Day 13, Day 23, Week 5, Week 9, Week 14, Week 26, Week 38. When finished, place your cards in your School Yard Science Notebook for further study.

P

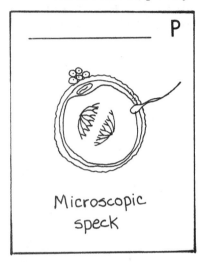

Microscopic speck

A

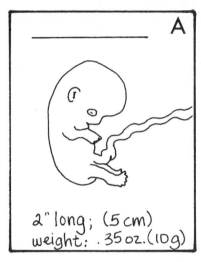

2" long; (5 cm) weight: .35 oz. (10g)

N₁

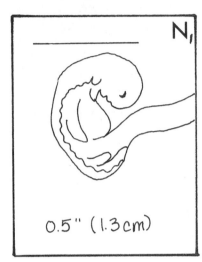

0.5" (1.3 cm)

R

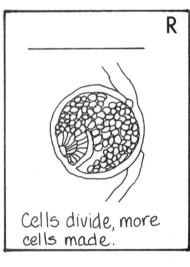

Cells divide, more cells made.

C

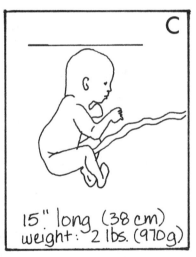

15" long (38 cm) weight: 2 lbs. (970g)

E

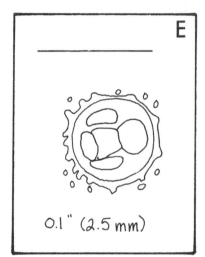

0.1" (2.5 mm)

Y

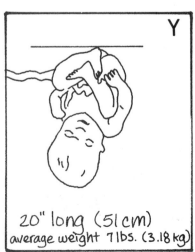

20" long (51 cm) average weight 7 lbs. (3.18 kg)

G

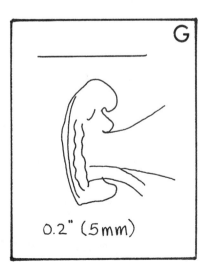

0.2" (5mm)

N₂

7" long (18 cm) weight: 4 oz. (113g)

94

GA1084

My First Life Cycle

PREGNANT

You were inside your **PREGNANT** mother for about nine months before you were born. Have you ever wondered how she felt during these nine months? Find out by interviewing your mother. Record what she says. Then with the help of your mother, write a news feature article like the one below that describes both of your experiences including your birth. Be sure to include information on who, what, where, when, why and how things happened.

After 2 months inside my mom, I am one thumb long from my head to my rump. I fit easily into a walnut shell. Everything about me is there and in place: my hands, feet, organs, and brain. My heart has been beating 150-175 times per minute for over one month already. At 9 months, I pushed out of my mother and began my own life. I am born to live life fully by being alive and happy.

GA1084

Feeling the Cycle of Adolescence to Adulthood

ADOLESCENCE is when a person grows from childhood to adulthood. Between ages 9 and 16, boys and girls experience changes in their bodies (see cards below). It is important to understand these changes because they affect your behavior. We get along better if we know how people change and feel as they do. Feelings change as your body changes. Check (✓) the box if you have experienced changes. Then cut out the cards below. Glue cards, in order, to a strip of cardboard. Carefully read the information on each card. Write the name of a person on each card who you know is at that stage of growth. Remember yourself. Place in your School Yard Science Notebook for further study.

Changes

Physical		Intellectual		Emotional		Social
Rapid Body Development		Can Think Logically		Anxiety Increase		Independent from Adults
Sex Organs Develop		Understands Weight and Volume		Feelings of Insecurity		Seek Peer (Friends') Approval
Blood Pressure and Pulse Rate Different		Creativity Changes		Often Tense		Need to Be More Sophisticated
Bones Grow Rapidly		Attention Span Increases		Often Restless		Boys Aggressive and Boisterous
Physical Endurance Increases		Reading Interests and Ability Change		Intense Enthusiasm		Girls Friendly and Neat

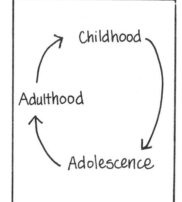

CHILDHOOD

A

Birth to Age 8
Boys and girls are immature physically and emotionally at this stage.

Name:

ADOLESCENCE

G

Ages 9 to 17
Boys and girls begin to mature physically and emotionally as the pituitary gland sends out hormones which stimulate growth of hair under arms, on legs and in the pubic area.

Name:

ADULTHOOD

E

Ages 18+
Men and women physically and emotionally mature at this stage.

Name:

GA1084

The Certificate of Adulthood

Many changes occur in people as they grow from childhood to ADULTHOOD. By talking with people, we can better understand these changes. Below are two certificates of adulthood. Interview two adults. Have them tell you about the physical and emotional changes that have occurred in them as they became adults. Record their responses on the certificates. Then think about, and circle, any of the same changes that have occurred in yourself during these times. Keep the certificate in a safe place. Add to the list of changes as you grow older. Share them with family members.

Certificate of Adulthood

Physical Changes:

Emotional Changes:

Certificate of Adulthood

Physical Changes:

Emotional Changes:

97

GA1084

O_2 + CO_2 = THE CYCLE OF LIFE

CO_2
O_2

Animals need plants to live and plants need animals to live. We all need each other to live. The oxygen-carbon dioxide cycle repeats itself over and over. It is basic to all life. Cut out the cycle of information. Tape Tab A to Tab B. Slide over 12-ounce juice can. Turn can to show how O_2 and CO_2 cycle repeats itself over and over again. Then study how people kill plants so they can build new buildings and highways on the land. Write a letter to your representative in Congress to explain how this practice affects the O_2 CO_2 cycle and life in general. Then make other cycle strips such as the "greenhouse" effect to be placed on your can for later study.

(TAB A)

AIR:
Nitrogen (N)
Carbon
   Dioxide (CO_2)
Oxygen (O_2)

Plants breathe
in CO_2

Sun helps
plants
make food

We breathe
IN
O_2

We breathe
OUT
CO_2

(TAB B)

GA1084

The Cycle of Breathing

RESPIRATION
DIAPHRAGM
INHALE
EXHALE

Our breathing cycle called **RESPIRATION** takes about six seconds. When we take air in (**INHALE**), a muscle called the **DIAPHRAGM** moves down. The outside air rushes into our lungs because they have less pressure in them. When we breathe out (**EXHALE**), the **DIAPHRAGM** moves up. It forces the air out of our lungs. The cycle is repeated about 10-16 times per minute depending upon our activity.

Study how your lungs work when you breathe. With scissors poke a hole near the bottom of a sturdy, plastic two or three-liter pop container. Cut off bottom. Insert straws and clay as shown. Add two balloons to flexible straws. Cut apart a punch ball balloon for **DIAPHRAGM**. Tape over opening in container. Pull **DIAPHRAGM** down. Observe size of balloons (lungs) inside container. Push **DIAPHRAGM** up. Observe size of balloons. Compare in and out cycle of breathing by pulling downward and pushing upward on the diaphragm. Then on the lungs below, write the number of times you breathe in one minute.

TIP: The life span of one breath is 3.75 seconds.

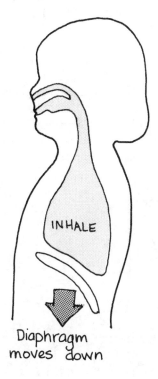

INHALE

Diaphragm moves down

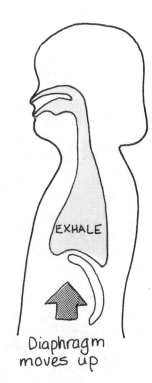

EXHALE

Diaphragm moves up

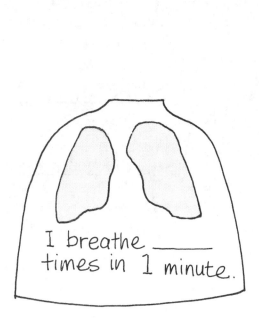

I breathe _____ times in 1 minute.

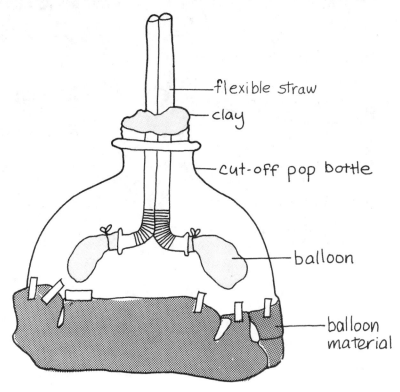

flexible straw

clay

cut-off pop bottle

balloon

balloon material

GA1084

The Cardiac Cycle

The HEART pumps blood throughout your body. Blood also flows through your HEART repeating this cycle many times per day. Sometimes blood looks bluish-red because most of its oxygen has been used. With a *blue* marker or pen, connect letters A-J to show the path of bluish-red blood in the HEART. The bluish-red blood then goes to the LUNGS to pick up oxygen. When it comes back to the HEART, it is bright red. With a *red* marker or pen, connect the letters K-U to show the flow of red blood. The red blood then takes food and oxygen to all parts of the body. The cycle begins again as bluish-red blood returns to the HEART. Place clear plastic over page. Move one drop of red and blue food coloring through heart to show circulation of blood through the heart. Then study the parts of the heart. Place in your School Yard Science Notebook for further study.

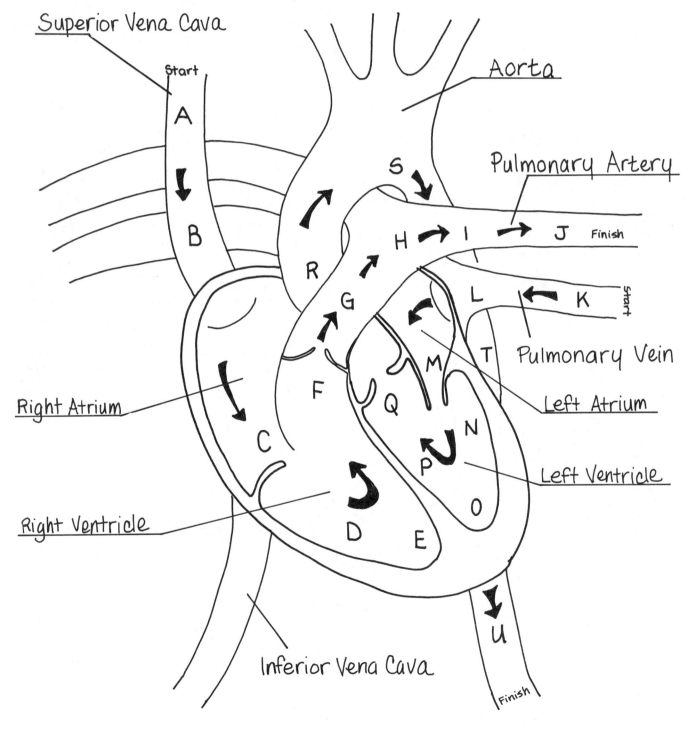

GA1084

Pulse Cycle

You can feel when the heart pumps blood through your body by taking your PULSE. First, mark an "X" on the drawing where you can feel your PULSE. At rest, count the number of times that your heart beats in one minute. Record. Run in place for one minute. Count again. Record number of beats in one minute. Subtract number of beats after exercise from number of beats at rest. What causes this difference? Then time how long it takes your heart to complete its cycle and return to its beginning PULSE rate. This is called "recovery time." Record all information on the heart below. Then take the PULSE of a *pet* at home. Compare to human pulse rate. Record your results in your Backyard Science Notebook.

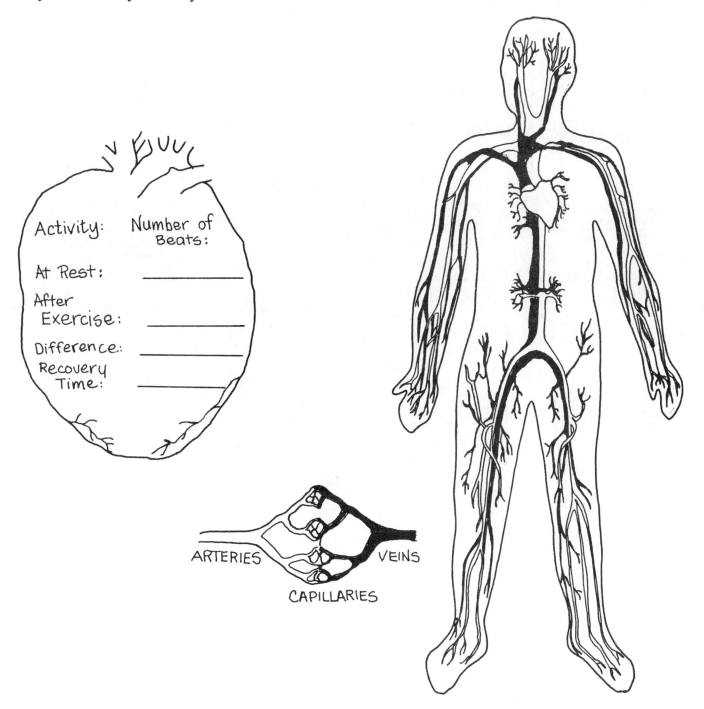

Activity: Number of
                  Beats:

At Rest: _____

After
  Exercise: _____

Difference: _____

Recovery
  Time: _____

ARTERIES   VEINS

CAPILLARIES

GA1084

Sleep Cycles

SLEEP is a time when people are not aware of their surroundings. Body activity is less, muscles relax and heart and breathing rates go down. The brain, however, remains very active. It gives off electrical waves in cycles, some of which last only one second. Below are five cards that show five different cycles of electrical waves given off by the front part of your brain during sleep. Using an encyclopedia and the list of words below, write the name on the card that best matches that four-second electrical wave. Then cut out and glue the cards, in order from awake to dreaming, to a strip of cardboard. Place in your School Yard Science Notebook for further study. Be sure to include a definition of the word ELECTROENCEPHALOGRAPHY.

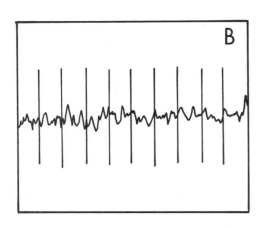

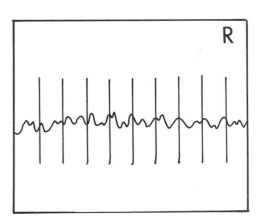

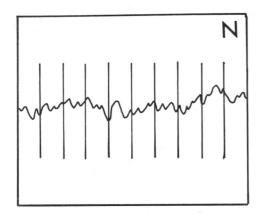

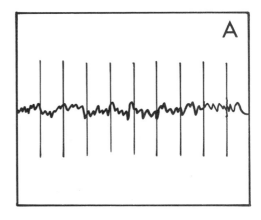

Electroencephalography is the_____

_____

Words to Choose from:
1. Awake but resting with eyes closed
2. Sleep begins
3. Deeper sleep
4. Deepest sleep
5. Dreaming

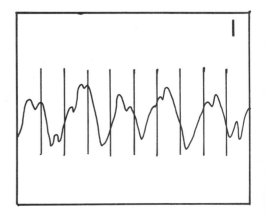

GA1084

Sleep/Wake Cycle

The sleep and wake cycle is called a CIRCADIAN cycle because it is a 24-hour pattern. People in our society follow a CIRCADIAN sleep/wake cycle of twenty-four hours with one period of sleep every night. Some people in other societies have two periods of sleep per day, a nap and regular sleep time. In the chart below, record the time each day you go to sleep, the time when you awaken, the total hours of sleep and your feelings for each day for one week. Post your chart on your bedroom door. Note the days when you sleep the most, least, and the latest and earliest times you go to bed. Compare each day's recordings to how you feel on that day. In your Backyard Science Notebook, write a story about how the amount of sleep affects your feelings.

TIP: The average number of hours of sleep for youngsters ages 10-13 is 10.

Day	Bedtime	Awake Time	Total Hours Slept	How I feel
Sunday				
Monday				
Tuesday				
Wednesday				
Thursday				
Friday				
Saturday				

GA1084

Birth to Advanced Age Cycle

After a baby is born, it continues to grow until it finishes its LIFE CYCLE on Earth. As the baby grows, it goes through stages. Below are twelve cards that show these stages. Cut out the cards, place in order and glue to cardboard. In the circle on each card, write the correct age for that person. Choose from ages 1, 3, 5, 7, 8, 10, 13, 18, 22, 40, 60 and 75. When finished, place your cards in your School Yard Science Notebook for further study.

D

W

G₂

O

R₂

O₂

E

N

R

G

L

I

104

GA1084

Life's Stages: an Ending, a Beginning

Below are pictures of twelve people at various stages in life. Their ages are found in the circles on each card for each person. With help from your family members, write the name below each STAGE of a person you know who is that age. Then ask members of your family what they feel the next STAGE in life will be after a person has completed all the stages in this life.

Biological Science Recycle

Recycling means that we can reuse many materials that we use once. We can recycle parts of our bodies so that others may live. Read the bumper sticker found on the rear bumper of the automobile below. Color in, circle, or "X" the number on the scale at the left that best tells your feelings about the message on the bumper sticker. With help from your teacher and parents, find out how and why people recycle parts of their bodies so others may live. Then draw your own bumper sticker that has as its message the recycling of your favorite body part. Place in your School Yard-Backyard Science Notebook for future use.

WHERE DO I STAND?	FOR
	10
	9
	8
	7
	6
	5
	4
	3
	2
	1
	AGAINST

HERE IS THE PLACE WHERE DEATH ENJOYS AIDING LIFE

LIFE: PASS IT ON
BE AN ORGAN DONOR +

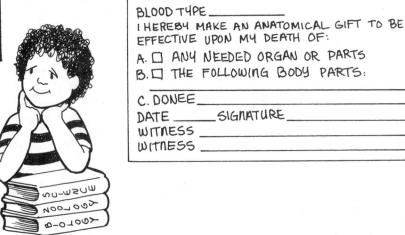

(Look on REVERSE side of driver's license)

BLOOD TYPE_____

I HEREBY MAKE AN ANATOMICAL GIFT TO BE EFFECTIVE UPON MY DEATH OF:

A. ☐ ANY NEEDED ORGAN OR PARTS
B. ☐ THE FOLLOWING BODY PARTS:
_____

C. DONEE_____
DATE _____ SIGNATURE_____
WITNESS _____
WITNESS _____

GA1084

School Yard(S)-Backyard(B) Physical Science Cycles

Here are some pictures of activities that you and your youngsters will encounter in this section.

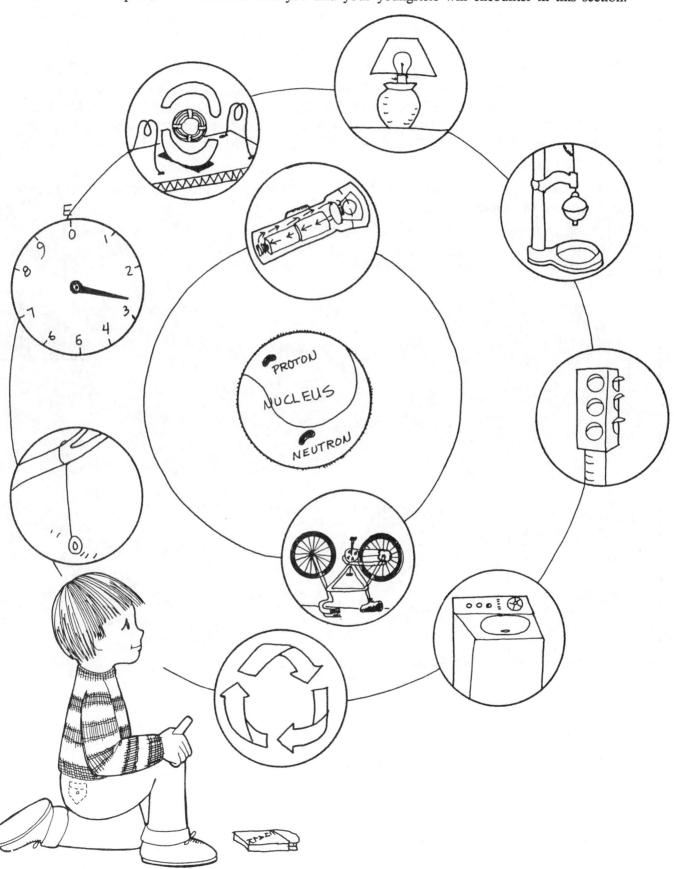

Electron Cycles

An ATOM is a basic unit of matter. The three basic parts of an ATOM are ELECTRONS, PROTONS and NEUTRONS. The PROTONS and NEUTRONS are found in the center of the ATOM called the NUCLEUS. The ELECTRONS cycle around the NUCLEUS in irregular paths called shells, many billion times per second. Each shell holds only a certain number of ELECTRONS. Go outside on the playground. Using chalk, draw the picture below on the playground. Place two tennis balls (PROTON, NEUTRON) inside the nucleus. Place two tiny pieces of gravel (ELECTRONS) in the K shell, 8 in the M shell and 32 in the N shell. O shell can hold 50 ELECTRONS, P shell 72 and Q shell 98 but these are rarely filled. Then have your friends, who wear different colored clothes, be the ELECTRONS, PROTONS and NEUTRONS. Have them act out the role of each part of the atom.

TIP: Be sure to make a drawing of the ATOM and its parts. Place in your School Yard Science Notebook for further study.

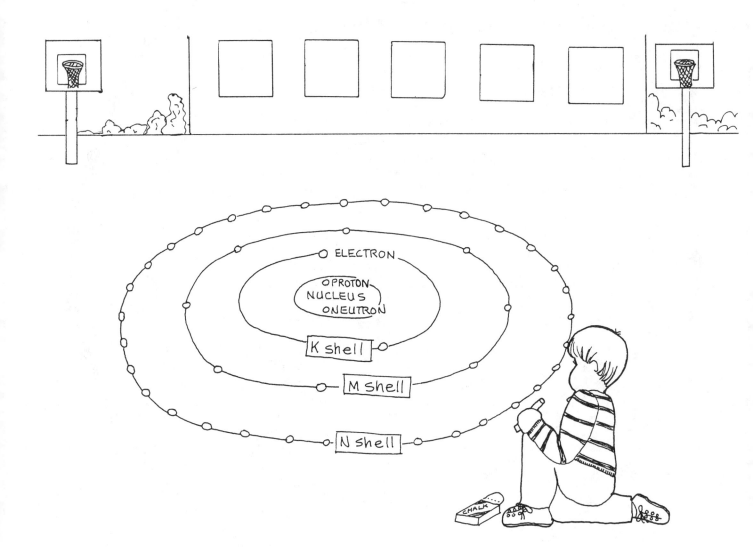

GA1084

Atomic Cycles

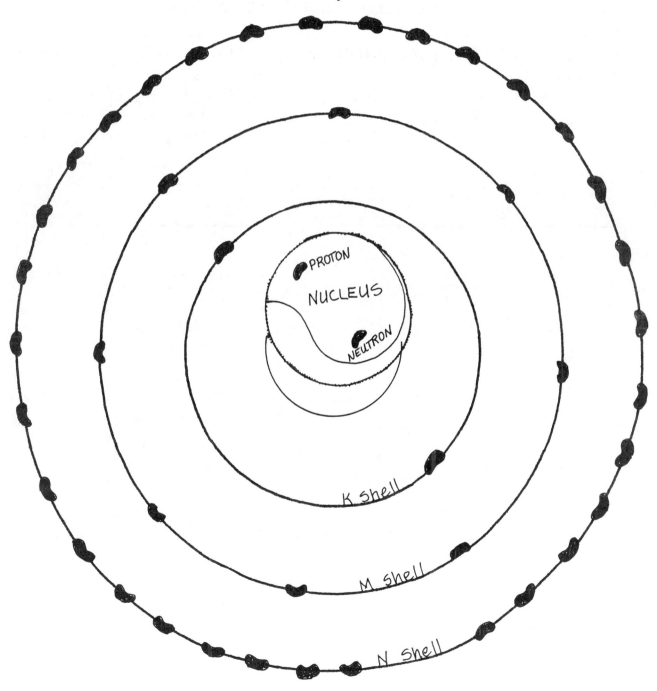

NUCLEUS
SHELL

With help from your parents, use a record player to study the parts of an atom. Cut out the circle below. Glue to single-layered cardboard. Punch hole in center. Place on record player. Punch hole in old tennis ball. Label this ball "NUCLEUS." Place on spindle of record player. Glue one light-colored seed (proton) and one dark-colored seed (neutron) to tennis ball (NUCLEUS). Glue seeds (electrons) on each shell. Hold tennis ball. Turn record player on low speed. Observe movement of seeds (electrons) in each SHELL as they travel around the tennis ball (NUCLEUS). In what direction do the electrons spin? Be sure to make a drawing of the atom. Label its parts. Place in your Backyard Science Notebook for further study.

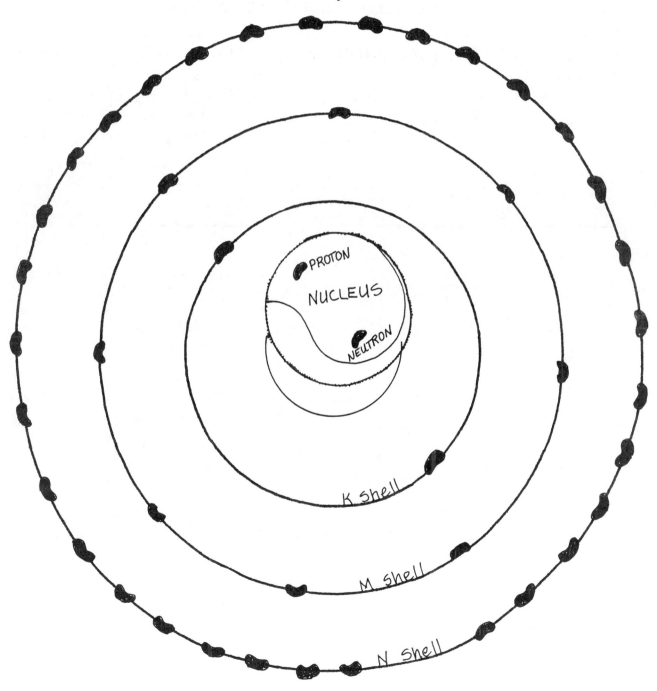

GA1084

60 Cycles

An electric CURRENT is a flow of electrical charges. This CURRENT can be of two types: DIRECT or ALTERNATING. DIRECT CURRENT (DC) always flows in the same direction. ALTERNATING CURRENT (AC) reverses its direction 60 times or CYCLES per second. When a coil of wire spins between the poles of a magnet, the CURRENT produced goes through one complete cycle. At the end of the cycle, the CURRENT changes direction to begin a new cycle. Below are four cards that show one cycle of ALTERNATING CURRENT. Cut out each card. Write 1, 2, 3, 4 in circles on matching card. Mount cards, in order, on a piece of stiff cardboard. Fold the paper below to show how electricity travels. Place in your School Yard Science Notebook for further study.

+

First quarter of spin: current builds up to maximum in one direction.

−

Second quarter of spin: current goes back to 0 and current changes direction.

~

Third quarter of spin: current builds up to maximum in the other direction.

~

Fourth quarter of spin: current goes back to zero, current changes direction, one spin completed, one cycle completed.

Fold this paper to show the flow of AC current.

FIRST QUARTER	SECOND QUARTER	THIRD QUARTER	FOURTH QUARTER
0 to Maximum	Maximum to 0	0 to Maximum	Maximum to 0 One Cycle Completed
In First DIRECTION	Current Changes DIRECTION	Other DIRECTION	*Does this 60 times per second.

fold fold fold

GA1084

DC or AC

DC current flows in one direction. AC current changes its direction twice in one cycle. The number of cycles per second is called FREQUENCY. The unit in which the FREQUENCY is measured is called HERTZ. Local power companies usually supply alternating current to your home with a FREQUENCY of 60 HERTZ. Below are pictures of objects that need electricity to run. With help from your parents, find the objects pictured on the cards below in your home. In the blank, write the letters "AC" if the object runs on alternating current, "DC" if it operates on direct current. Then use your glossary to find out what the terms RECTIFIER and TRANSFORMER mean. Place this sheet along with your findings in your Backyard Science Notebook for further study.

GA1084

Circuit Cycles

An electric CIRCUIT is a closed path of electrical current. Electricity must flow in a closed CIRCUIT to do work. In a closed CIRCUIT the electricity travels in a complete cycle from a source such as a dry cell, through a connector such as a wire to an output device like a lamp, then through the wire returning to the dry cell. Below are twelve pictures of various CIRCUITS. Use dry cells, flashlight bulb and piece of wire to find out if the bulb will or will not light. Guess first by circling *will light* or *won't light*. Try out. Record results. Cut out cards. Mount cards on two different pieces of cardboard, one labeled "will light," the other "won't light." Keep in your School Yard Science Notebook for further use.

A

Guess: Will light.
            Won't light.

Try Out: It lit.
          It didn't
          light.

Results: Correct
          Incorrect

B

Guess: Will light.
            Won't light.

Try Out: It lit.
          It didn't
          light.

Results: Correct
          Incorrect

C

Guess: Will light.
            Won't light.

Try Out: It lit.
          It didn't
          light.

Results: Correct
          Incorrect

D

Guess: Will light.
            Won't light.

Try Out: It lit.
          It didn't
          light.

Results: Correct
          Incorrect

E

Guess: Will light.
            Won't light.

Try Out: It lit.
          It didn't
          light.

Results: Correct
          Incorrect

F

Guess: Will light.
            Won't light.

Try Out: It lit.
          It didn't
          light.

Results: Correct
          Incorrect

G

Guess: Will light.
            Won't light.

Try Out: It lit.
          It didn't
          light.

Results: Correct
          Incorrect

H

Guess: Will light.
            Won't light.

Try Out:
It lit.
It didn't
light.

Results: Correct
          Incorrect

I

Guess: Will light.
            Won't light.

Try Out: It lit.
          It didn't
          light.

Results: Correct
          Incorrect

J

Guess: Will light.
            Won't light.

Try Out: It lit.
          It didn't
          light.

Results: Correct
          Incorrect

K

Guess: Will light.
            Won't light.

Try Out: It lit.
          It didn't
          light.

Results: Correct
          Incorrect

L

Guess: Will light.
            Won't light.

Try Out: It lit.
          It didn't
          light.

Results: Correct
          Incorrect

GA1084

Flashlight Circuit Cycle

When a flashlight works, electric CURRENT flows in a complete path through the flashlight. With help from your parents, take apart, then put together a flashlight. Turn on flashlight. Observe brightness. With a pen, connect the arrows on the flashlight below to show the path of electricity. Then remove the dry cells from the flashlight. Find out what happens when one dry cell is turned around. Be sure to observe how the flip of the switch makes a light glow in a flashlight. Answer the questions below. Keep in your Backyard Science Notebook for further study.

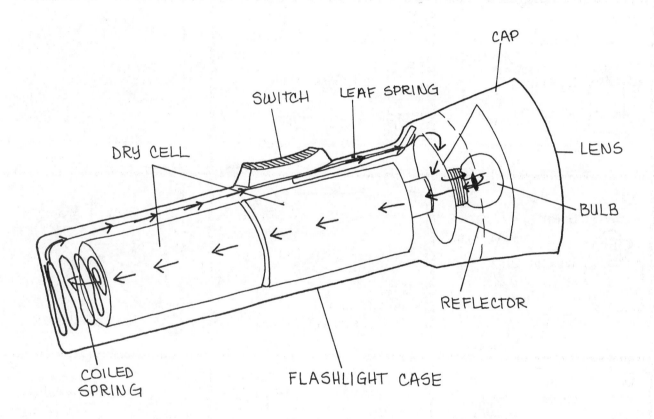

QUESTIONS:

1. What happens when you place one dry cell in the opposite direction in the flashlight?

_____

2. How does the flip of the switch make the light glow in a flashlight?

_____

Electrical Cycles at School

In school, youngsters study things about ELECTRICITY such as basic electrical circuits. Study the cards below. Circle the word that best describes the picture correctly. Then compare the pictures on this page with those on page 115. How are they alike? How are they different? Cut out the cards. Match cards to those on page 115. Play concentration with a friend.

1 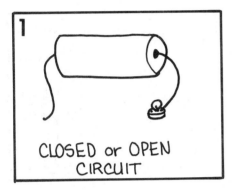 CLOSED or OPEN CIRCUIT	**2** 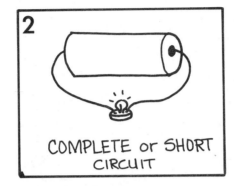 COMPLETE or SHORT CIRCUIT	**3** STATIC or CURRENT ELECTRICITY 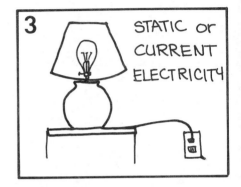
4 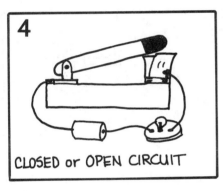 CLOSED or OPEN CIRCUIT	**5** 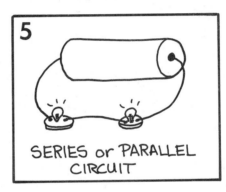 SERIES or PARALLEL CIRCUIT	**6** 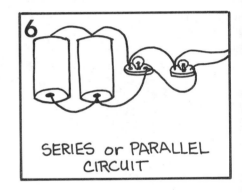 SERIES or PARALLEL CIRCUIT
7 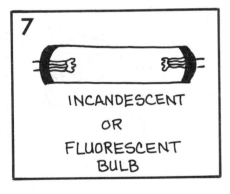 INCANDESCENT OR FLUORESCENT BULB	**8** 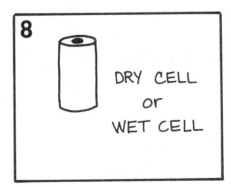 DRY CELL or WET CELL	**9** CONDUCTOR or INSULATOR 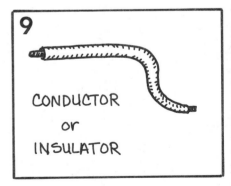
10 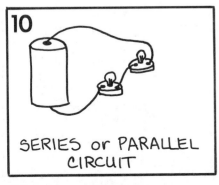 SERIES or PARALLEL CIRCUIT	**11** 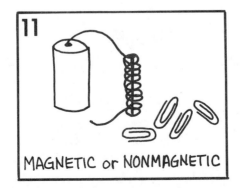 MAGNETIC or NONMAGNETIC	**12**  MOTOR or GENERATOR

GA1084

Electrical Cycles at Home

Youngsters can OBSERVE many objects at home that use electricity. OBSERVE the drawings below. Circle the word that best describes the picture correctly. Then compare these pictures with those on page 114. How are they alike? How are they different? Cut out the cards. Match the cards with those on page 114. Play concentration with a friend.

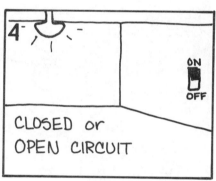

1 — OPEN or CLOSED CIRCUIT

2 — COMPLETE or SHORT CIRCUIT

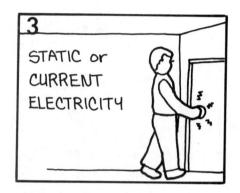

3 — STATIC or CURRENT ELECTRICITY

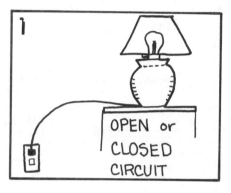

4 — CLOSED or OPEN CIRCUIT

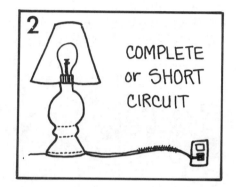

5 — SERIES or PARALLEL CIRCUIT

6 — SERIES or PARALLEL CIRCUIT

7 — INCANDESCENT or FLUORESCENT BULB

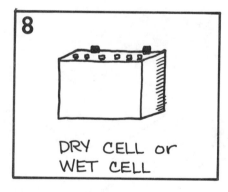

8 — DRY CELL or WET CELL

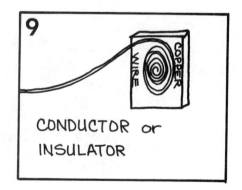

9 — CONDUCTOR or INSULATOR

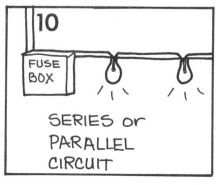

10 — FUSE BOX — SERIES or PARALLEL CIRCUIT

11 — MAGNETIC or NONMAGNETIC

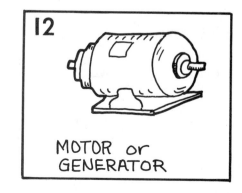

12 — MOTOR or GENERATOR

115

GA1084

Electric Meter Cycles at School

An electric meter measures electric current used in KILOWATT hours (kWh). A KILOWATT hour is 1000 watt hours. Electric meters are read at regular times. The customer's bill is based on these readings. Below is a picture of one electric meter. Read the number of KILOWATT hours (kWh) shown on the dials.

TIP: Electric meter dials are read right to left from ones, tens, hundreds, thousands and ten thousands. The pointer on dial A must make one complete cycle for the pointer on dial B to move ahead one unit. The process goes on and on. If the hand is between two numbers, read it as the lower number. Write the number of KILOWATT hours shown on the dials in the blank below. You are now ready to take your practice dials home and read your electric meter.

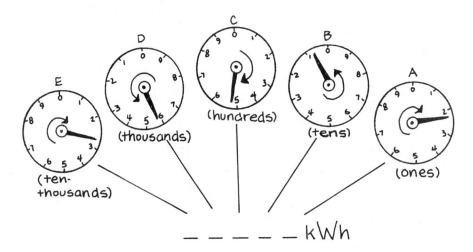

_ _ _ _ _ _ kWh

I am _____

Number of KILOWATT hours shown on meter: _____

116

GA1084

Electric Meter Cycles at Home

Reading your electric meter regularly at home helps you find out how much electricity in kilowatt hours (kWh) is being used. Below are sample pages on which you and your parents can record how much electricity you use per day. Read electric meter each day for one week. Draw location of arrows on dials below. Record today's reading. Repeat for day two. Find daily usage (subtract day one's reading from day two's reading). Then make a bar graph below that shows how much electricity was used each day for one week.

My Book of Home Electricity Use

Name _____
School _____

Today's Reading _____ kWh
Yesterday's Reading _____ kWh
Total kWh Used _____

Date: _____

Today's Reading _____ kWh
Yesterday's Reading _____ kWh
Total kWh Used _____

Date: _____

Today's Reading _____ kWh
Yesterday's Reading _____ kWh
Total kWh Used _____

Date: _____

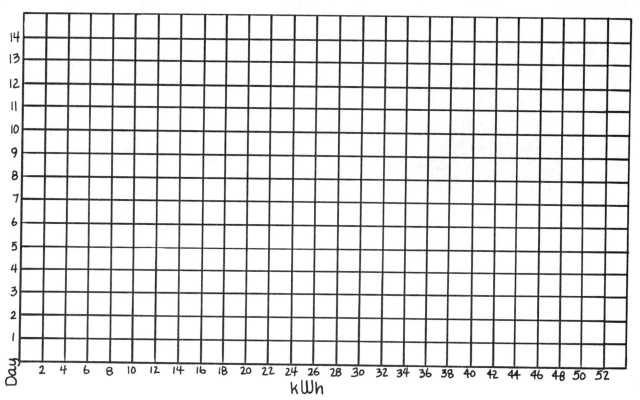

Electric Motor Cycles at School

Electric motors make many revolutions or cycles per minute. They change electrical energy into mechanical **POWER** to do work. Motors work because flowing electric current produces a magnetic field. Set up magnetic fields so one magnet spins inside another magnet as shown below. Study the picture of the motor on Card 3. Gouge out hole in triple-wall, wood or hold magnet in place with clay. Make two support wire loops (Card 1). Attach to triple-wall or wood with thumbtacks as shown on Card 1. Next make a coil of wire, called an **ARMATURE**, shown on Card 2. Place coil of wire in loops as shown on Card 3. Hook up dry cell to loops. Hold magnet on top of coil. What happens? Why? Turn top magnet 90^0, 180^0. What happens? Why? Try to count number of revolutions or cycles that your motor makes in one minute. Place magnets in different positions. Record what you found out in your School Yard Science Notebook.

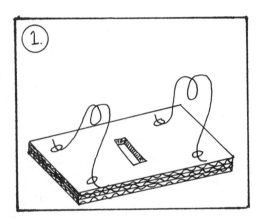

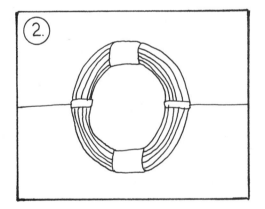

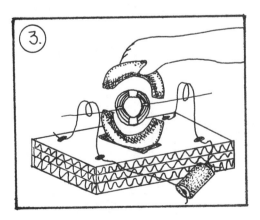

GA1084

Electric Motor Cycles at Home

Motors run many appliances in your home. In a chart like the one below, make a list of all home appliances powered by motors. With help from your parents, read the information tag on the motor to find its AMPS and VOLTS. Find the total amount of electrical energy consumed by the motor in kilowatts by multiplying the current in AMPS by the voltage in VOLTS by the time in hours and dividing by 1000. The first one, vacuum cleaner, is done for you. A 3-AMP vacuum cleaner running one hour on 120 VOLTS uses .36 kilowatt-hours of energy. Then contact your local power company. Find out the current rate per kilowatt-hour. Figure your monthly bill per motor. Try to reduce the amount of electricity you use as each day goes by. Energy conservation saves money and natural resources.

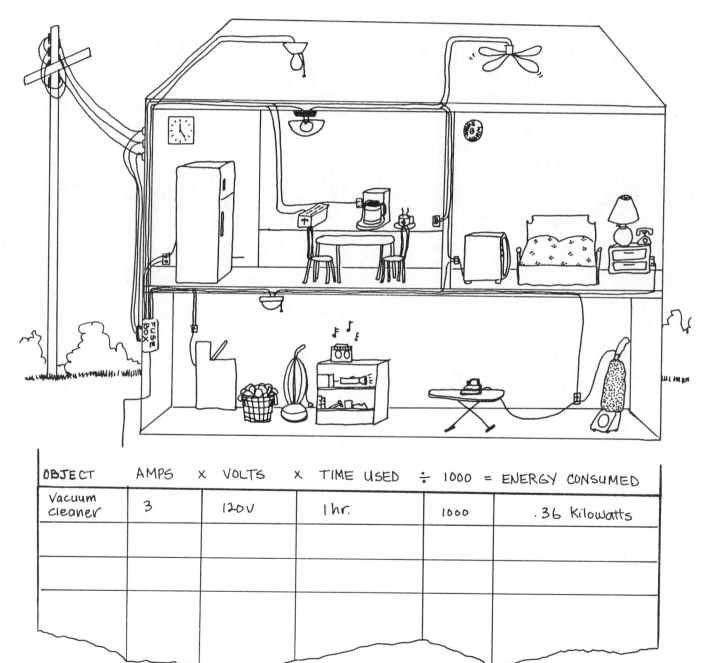

OBJECT	AMPS	x VOLTS	x TIME USED	÷ 1000	= ENERGY CONSUMED
Vacuum cleaner	3	120V	1 hr.	1000	.36 Kilowatts

GA1084

Cycle of a Traffic Light at School

TRAFFIC lights guide motor vehicles and people in TRAFFIC. TRAFFIC flows smoothly when TRAFFIC lights are used because their cycles can be set as the TRAFFIC demand increases or decreases. Below are five pictures of various phases in the cycle of a TRAFFIC light. Color Card A the colors found on a TRAFFIC light. Color Card B the color for stop; Card C "go," D "caution," E "stop." Cut out cards. Mount on a stiff piece of cardboard. Read about the works of Garrett Morgan. Write a letter on the cardboard about changes in stoplights since his time like "left turn on green arrow" and "right turn after stop when light is on red."

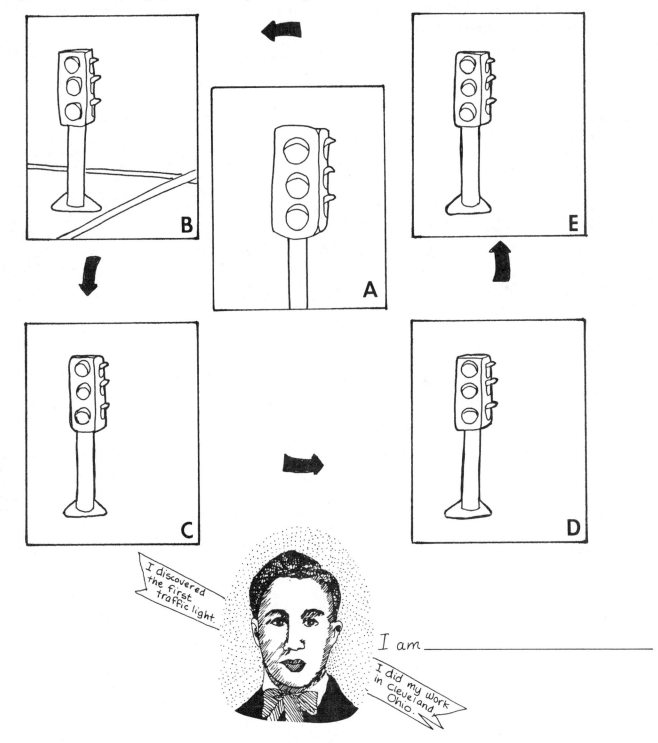

I discovered the first traffic light.

I did my work in Cleveland, Ohio.

I am _____

GA1084

Cycle of a Traffic Light at Intersection

The cycle of modern traffic lights is set according to traffic demands. Some traffic lights go through their cycles in a few seconds, others in minutes, depending upon the amount of traffic. Some traffic lights have a button on them that, when pushed, allows people to cross busy streets safely. With help from your parents, observe two traffic lights found at two different INTERSECTIONS. Time how long it takes each traffic light to complete one cycle change from red to green, green to yellow, and yellow to red. Record the time of day, amount of traffic and cycle time in the blanks below. Do the same but at a different time during the day. Compare your results. When is traffic the heaviest? Lightest? Listen to reports from a traffic copter. Record what you found out in your Backyard Science Notebook.

TIP: Fully installed traffic lights remain for fifteen to twenty years. Some are updated before this time.

Intersection 1

Intersection 2

Intersection 1

Time of Day _____

Cycle Time: _____

Traffic: Light _____

Medium _____

Heavy _____

Intersection 2

Time of Day _____

Cycle Time: _____

Traffic: Light _____

Medium _____

Heavy _____

GA1084

Pendulum Cycles at School

A pendulum is an object that swings back and forth from a fixed point. A swing is a pendulum. The path traveled by the swing is called an ARC. The time it takes the swing to pass back and forth *once* over this ARC is its PERIOD. Go outside on the playground. Observe a swing. Note how it is attached to a fixed point. Push swing forward. Note the ARC of the pendulum. Then push the swing forward and let it return to you. This full cycle is called the PERIOD. Time how long it takes for an empty swing to go one cycle back and forth. Then ride the swing for one cycle. Do not pump. Record time. Does adding your weight to the swing cause the pendulum to travel faster and have a greater number of PERIODS? Record your findings in your School Yard Science Notebook. Then using an encyclopedia, read about how Galileo discovered the laws of the pendulum.

I discovered the laws of the pendulum when I was age 20.

From observing a swinging lamp,

I am _____

GA1084

Swinging Cycles at Home

BOB

With help from your parents, build a pendulum in your backyard. Hang a vertical length of fishline from a low tree branch. Hang a weight such as a metal nut on the end of the string. This weight is called the BOB of the pendulum. Let the pendulum swing. Observe the arc and period of the pendulum. Measure the length of the fishline. Count the number of periods the pendulum makes in one minute. Change the length of the string. Count the number of periods. Change the weight of the BOB. Count the number of periods. Answer the questions below. Make a list of other pendulums found in your home. Place in your Backyard Science Notebook.

QUESTIONS:

1. What effect does the weight of the BOB have on the number of periods of the pendulum?

_____

2. What effect does the length of the fishline have on the number of periods of the pendulum?

_____

GA1084

Bicycle Cycles

Bicycles are used for recreation and transportation. The wheels on a bicycle make many REVOLUTIONS or cycles per minute. Before you can understand how many REVOLUTIONS or cycles a bicycle makes, you need to know its parts and how it works. Write the number of the part in each space below. Then study how Wilbur Wright developed the bicycle.

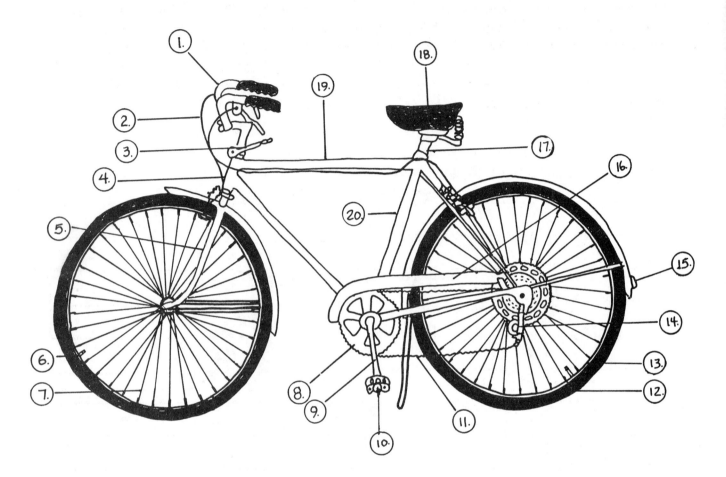

	Steering Head		Brake Lever
	Fork		Air Valve
	Pedal		Chainwheel
	Handlebars		Brake Cable
	Rim		Tire
	Top Tube		Spoke
	Rear Derailleur		Rear Reflector
	Seat Post		Chain Guard
	Seat Tube		Seat or Saddle
	Crank		Chain

I like to ride bicycles and fly airplanes.

I am _____

GA1084

Pedal Power

You push on PEDALS to make a bicycle move. The PEDALS turn a SPROCKET which has a chain that turns a smaller SPROCKET on the rear wheel. Some bicycles have additional GEARS for different speeds. A ten-speed bicycle has two GEARS on the CHAINWHEEL and five GEARS on the rear wheel. These GEARS give the bike its ten different speeds.

At home, turn your bicycle upside down. Tie a string between two spokes around the rear wheel. Using the PEDALS, turn the CHAINWHEEL one complete turn. Observe how many times the rear wheel turns. Repeat by using a bicycle that has different speeds. Record your results in the chart below. How is the number of turns of the rear wheel related to the number of turns of the CHAINWHEEL for different GEARS? Show your results to members of your family. Then compare one speed to ten-speed bicycles. Which one has a greater number of cycles?

Speed	Number of Chainwheel Turns	Number of Rear Wheel Turns	Observations

GA1084

Four-Stroke Cycle Gasoline Engine

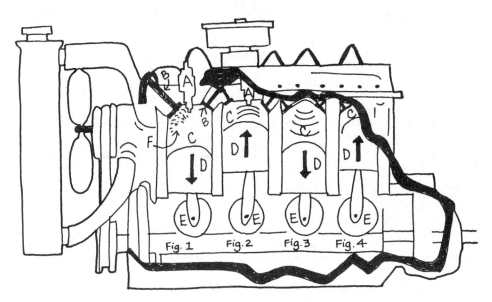

A gasoline engine, called an internal combustion engine, produces power by burning a mixture of gasoline vapor and air inside a CYLINDER. All gasoline engines have either a two or four-stroke cycle. Pictured below is a four-cylinder, four-cycle gasoline engine. Locate (A) spark plug, (B) intake valve, (C) cylinder, (D) piston, (E) crankshaft and (F) fuel-air mixture. Observe the position of the piston during the intake stroke (Figure 1), the compression stroke (Figure 2), power stroke (Figure 3) and exhaust stroke (Figure 4). Cut out the cards below. Carefully read the information on each card. Number the cards to show the correct sequence of events. Glue or staple the cards, in order, to a strip of cardboard. Then with a friend, put fists in air. Make fists go up and down like the four pistons in a four-cyclinder, four-cycle engine. Be sure the timing of your "engine" is correct.

Fig. 1   Fig. 2   Fig. 3   Fig. 4

○ Piston moves down cylinder.	○ Piston moves up cylinder the second time.	○ Spark-plug ignites mixture.
○ Exhaust valve opens.	○ Intake valve opens.	○ Burned gases push piston down.
○ Burned gases pushed out by piston.	○ Fuel-air mixture drawn into cylinder.	○ Piston moves up cylinder first time and squeezes fuel-air mixture.

GA1084

Two or Four-Stroke
Cycle Gasoline Engines

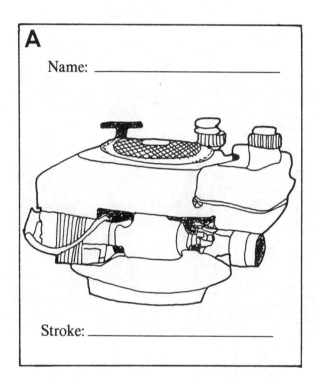

STROKE

Gasoline engines are often used around the home to do work. Below are pictures of both lawn mower and automobile gasoline engines. With help from your parents at home, inspect both of these engines. Then on the cards below, print the name, lawn mower or automobile. Tell whether the engine is a two or four-STROKE cycle gasoline engine. To learn more about how engines work, interview an automobile mechanic to learn how a *diesel* engine works. Record what the mechanic said in your Backyard Science Notebook.

A

Name: _____

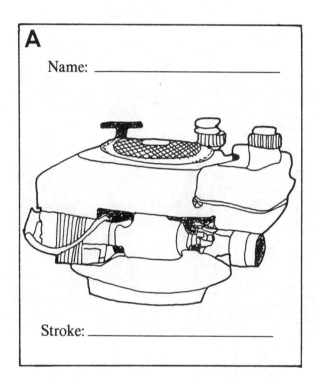

Stroke: _____

B

Name: _____

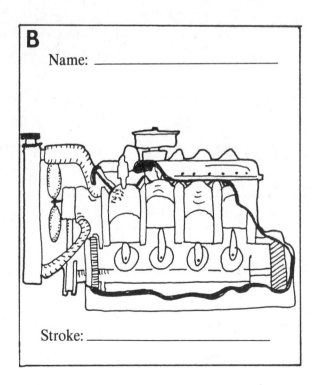

Stroke: _____

GA1084

Toilet Cycles at School

A toilet is used to flush wastes away into a sewer. When one pushes down on the handle, the water flushes out the wastes and fresh water comes in to refill the bowl. Number the pictures below to show the cycle of the toilet. Then cut out and mount the cards in order to a strip of cardboard. Look up information in an encyclopedia about Thomas Crapper. For what is he famous? Place the cards and related information in your schoolbag to be used at home in your further study.

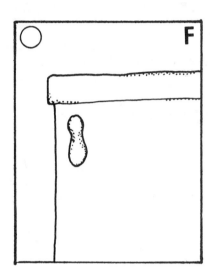

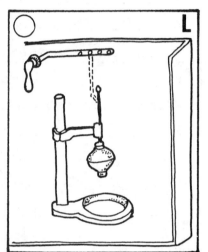

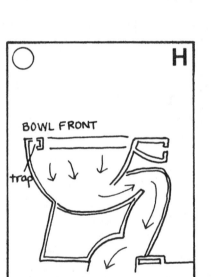

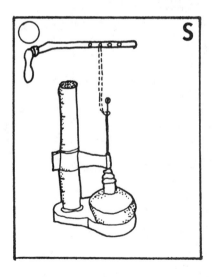

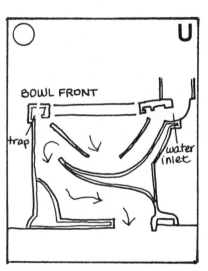

GA1084

Toilet Cycles at Home

The cycle of a toilet is interesting to study. With help from your parents, carefully observe and time each part of this cycle. Place a check mark in the blank as you complete each step.

1. _____ Remove lid from tank.

2. _____ Observe level of water.

3. _____ Observe STOPPER ball.

4. _____ Push down on handle.

5. _____ Observe how lift wire lifts stopper ball from flush VALVE SEAT.

6. _____ Observe water as it leaves tank and goes into toilet bowl.

7. _____ Observe water as it enters toilet bowl through little holes under rim of bowl.

8. _____ Observe stopper ball fall back into place in tank.

9. _____ Observe refilling of tank.

10. _____ Count the time in seconds that it takes to complete the cycle.

_____ Number of seconds to complete steps 9-10 above.

_____ Number of gallons (liters) of water used in one flushing.

GA1084

Washing Machine Cycles

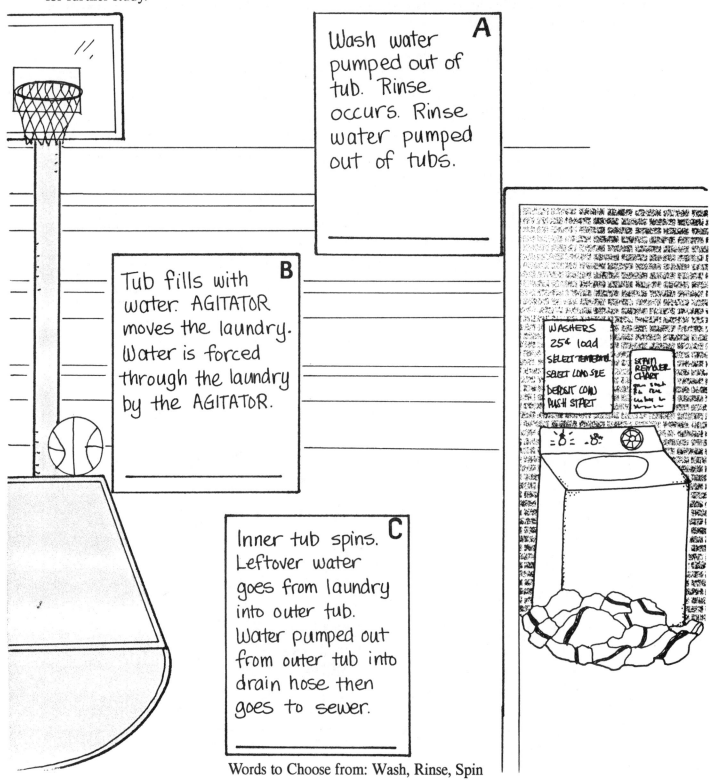

AGITATOR

A washing machine washes clothes very quickly. Most washing machines are automatic. You put in the clothes, detergent, and set the controls. Below are three cards that show the main phases in a complete washing cycle. Using the words below, write the correct name of the phase on each card. Cut out cards. Mount on a stiff piece of cardboard. Place in your schoolbag to take home for further study.

A

Wash water pumped out of tub. Rinse occurs. Rinse water pumped out of tubs.

B

Tub fills with water. AGITATOR moves the laundry. Water is forced through the laundry by the AGITATOR.

C

Inner tub spins. Leftover water goes from laundry into outer tub. Water pumped out from outer tub into drain hose then goes to sewer.

WASHERS 25¢ load SELECT TEMPERATURE SELECT LOAD SIZE DEPOSIT COIN PUSH START

STAIN REMOVER CHART

Words to Choose from: Wash, Rinse, Spin

130

GA1084

Automatic Washer Cycles

With help from your parents, study the CONTROL PANEL of the washing machine at home. The CONTROL PANEL has the names of automatic cycles for your washer. Wash a load of laundry with your parents' help. Complete the chart below by writing in the number of minutes for wash, rinse and spin phases for each of the five automatic wash cycles.

Be sure to ask your parents where the wash water goes once the cycle is over. This may lead you into your front or backyard for further study.

AUTOMATIC WASHER CYCLES

		Wash	Wash Time __minutes	Rinse	Rinse Time __minutes	Spin	Spin Time __minutes
1.	Regular		__minutes		__minutes		__minutes
2.	Perm Press		__minutes		__minutes		__minutes
3.	Delicates		__minutes		__minutes		__ minutes
4.	Knits		__minutes		__minutes		__minutes
5.	Soak		__minutes		__minutes		__minutes

GA1084

The Physical Science Cycle
of Recyling

Every day, people throw away many leftover, worn out, and broken things. These things are thrown into open dumps, burned in incinerators or put in a sanitary landfill and covered with soil by bulldozers. There is a need to reduce SOLID WASTE. One way to do this is by recycling which means we reuse things rather than throwing them away. Aluminum cans, glass and paper can be made into new things. Plus, you can make money doing it. Call the nearest recycling plant near you. Ask for information on prices for recyclable items. Write the information in the chart below. Place chart in your Backyard Science Notebook for future use. Then recycle as many items as you can. Get others involved in an effort to reduce SOLID WASTE.

MY RECYCLING CENTER'S

PHONE NUMBER:

_____

ADDRESS:

_____

_____

PRICES PAID FOR:

ALUMINUM CANS:

_____¢ per lb.

PAPER:

_____¢ per lb.

GLASS:

_____¢ per lb.

GLASS

ALUMINUM

GA1084

Part Three
Ongoing Special Projects and Ideas
Cycle of Science Magnetic Bulletin Board:
The Scientific Method

This bulletin board tells what scientists do. Attach magnetic tape to backs of cards. If you have a magnetic chalkboard, the cards will adhere to the chalkboard. If not, any metal surface from a discarded washer, dishwasher, refrigerator or clothes dryer will work. Have youngsters put the cards in order on the bulletin board to show what scientists do when using the scientific method. Then use the method often in your everyday life.

① Scientists ask questions like "What is the problem?" ? ? ?

② Scientists gather evidence by reading what others have written, listening to others and finding out what they have done.

⑥ A new problem comes up. Scientists ask more questions. These questions lead to more questions. ? ?

Scientific Method Card

1. State the problem in question form
2. Research the problem
3. State the procedure
4. Observe safe lab procedures
5. Predict outcome of experiment
6. Conduct experiment
   a. change conditions
   b. change one variable
7. Collect data
8. Identify results of experiment
   a. diagram
   b. flow chart
   c. paragraph(s)
9. Construct graphs
10. Analyze data
11. Compare data
12. Synthesize hypothesis
13. Draw conclusions
14. Discuss experiment with others
15. Write results using correct spelling and grammar

③ Scientists make a guess called a HYPOTHESIS before they begin their actual work with materials.

④ Scientists do trials called EXPERIMENTS which include observation and recording of information.

⑤ Scientists try to find out if the hypothesis was correct by writing a tentative CONCLUSION.

GA1084

Fifty-Two Card Deck
of
Science Cycles

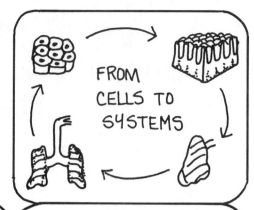
FROM CELLS TO SYSTEMS

D

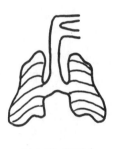

CELLS

N

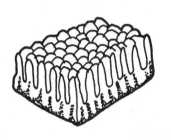

TISSUE

A

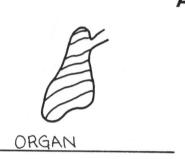

ORGAN

R

SYSTEM

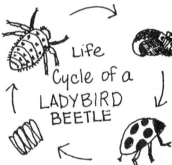
Life Cycle of a LADYBIRD BEETLE

LA

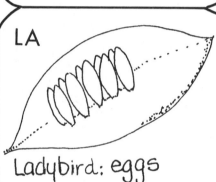

Ladybird: eggs

DY

Ladybird: Larva

BI

Ladybird: Pupa

RD

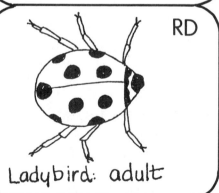

Ladybird: adult

Life Cycle of a Mosquito

R

Mosquito: Egg raft

A

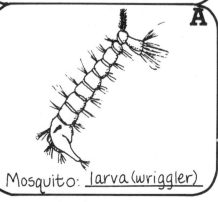

Mosquito: larva (wriggler)

134

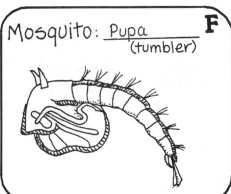

DIRECTIONS: Cut out the card deck of 52 cycle cards. Place each cycle in order. You should have 12 complete cycles when you are finished with your work.

Good luck!

T

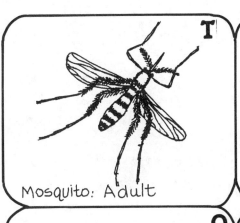

Mosquito: Adult

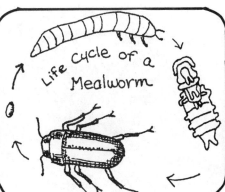

Life Cycle of a Mealworm

M

Mealworm: Egg

O

Mealworm: Larva

L

Mealworm: Pupa

T

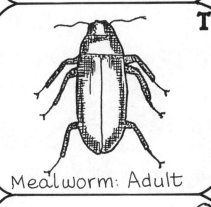

Mealworm: Adult

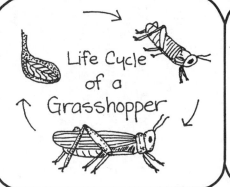

Life Cycle of a Grasshopper

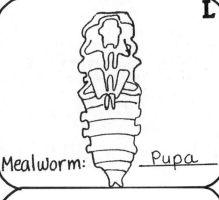

Grasshopper: Egg

Grasshopper: Nymph

Grasshopper: Adult

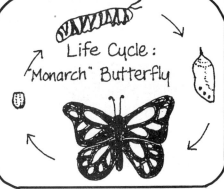

Life Cycle: "Monarch" Butterfly

MI

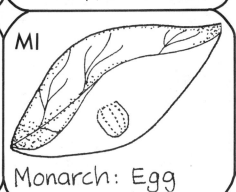

Monarch: Egg

135

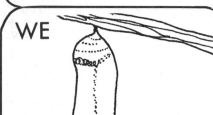

Monarch: caterpillar

WE

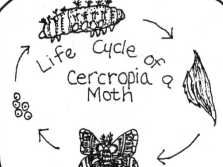

Monarch: Chrysalis

ED

Monarch: Adult

Life Cycle of Cercropia Moth

M

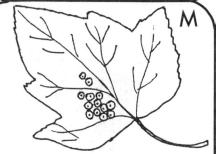

Cercropia moth: eggs

O

Cercropia moth: larva

T

Cercropia moth: cocoon

H

Cercropia moth: Adult

LIFE CYCLE OF A FROG

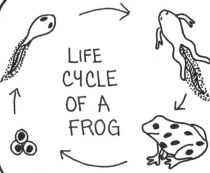

L

Frog: Eggs _____

E

Frog: tadpole without legs

A

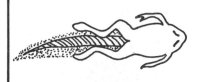

Frog: tadpole with legs

P

Frog: Adult

Life Cycle of an Apple Tree

P Apple Tree: Dormant

O Apple Tree: Blossom

M Apple Tree: Fruit set

E Apple Tree: Ripe fruit

Waxing Crescent

First Quarter

Waning Gibbcus

Full Moon

Waning Gibbous

Last Quarter

Waning Crescent

New Moon

GA1084

Slider Question and Answer Cycles Board

You will need a copy of the slider frame master (page 139), scissors, oaktag, glue, tape and slider. Begin by making copies of the slider frame (page 139) and slider (page 140) for each student. Mount on oaktag. Cut out two windows and thumb notch in slider frame. Fold tabs A and B on dotted lines towards back side of frame. Tape tabs together where they meet on the back of the slider frame. Insert slider A into slider frame. Read word(s) in window one and matching response in window two. Discuss responses. Have youngsters quiz each other. Then have students make their own sliders that feature science words or questions with matching responses on a cycle of science. Discuss the content of each newly created slider.

TIP: Encourage students to make sliders that feature in-depth questions and answers. On the slider, have students position answer that will appear in window two, one space above or below window one so answer will not appear directly across from window one. Also, encourage students to make sliders that have more than two windows.

Sliders of Science

138

SLIDER FRAME MASTER

TAB A

FOLD HERE

FOLD HERE

TAB B

Window One   Window Two

GA1084

SLIDER A
"CYCLES"

The Reuse of Things Found in Wastes	Recycle
Life Cycle of a White Blood Cell	12 Days
Life Cycle of a Red Blood Cell	120 Days
Life Cycle of a Liver Cell	540 Days
Life Cycle of a Nerve Cell	100 Years
A Plant That Has More Than a Two-Year Cycle	Perennial
Number of Hours in a Circadian Rhythm	24 Hours
Number of Tons of Soil an Earthworm Digests in One Year	36 Tons
Number of Years to Form One Inch (2.5 cm) of Soil	500 Years
Number of Days for Voyager to Orbit the Earth	9 Days
Number of Minutes for Space Shuttle to Orbit the Earth	75 Minutes
Number of Days to Travel Around an Analemma	365 1/4 Days (One Year)
Moon's Period of Revolution Around the Earth	One Month (30 Days)
Earth's Period of Rotation on Its Axis	One Day (24 Hours)
Earth's Period of Revolution Around the Sun	One Year (365 1/4 Days)
Mars' Period of Revolution Around the Sun	687 Days
Times During Which Certain Events Repeat Themselves	Cycle

Pull

GA1084

Part Four
Answers

pp. viii-ix
Left to right:
   Set A: 7, 6, 8, 17, 23
   Set B: 18, 13, 24, 4, 1
   Set C: 9, 25, 19, 5, 2
   Set D: 10, 26, 14, 3, 20
   Set E: 15, 27, 21, 11, 29
   Set F: 30, 16, 22, 12, 28

p. 17—Knowledge: B, D, D; Comprehension: A, C, D; Application: C, B, B; Analysis: B, D, C; Synthesis: C, A, D; Evaluation: A, C, A
pp. 21-22

Student Book—front cover

Student Book—back cover

p. 26—C O_1 S M O_2 L O_3 G I S_2 T S_3

p. 27—B_1 I G_1 B_2 A_1 N G_2 I_2 S_1 A_2 L_1 L_2 T_1 H A_3 T_2 M A_4 T_3 T_4 E R S_2

p. 28—(1) 33,000 LY, (2) 100,000 LY

p. 29—(1) 2, (2) 50,000 LY, (3) 33, 000 LY, (4) 8000 LY

p. 30—Supernova

p. 31—Sun's temperature: 6000⁰ K; sun's class and color: class G2, color yellow; star hotter: Orion 25,000⁰ K, color blue; star cooler: Betelgeuse 3000⁰ K, color red

p. 32

Word in Saying	Class	Example:	Approximate Temp.	Color
"Oh	O5	No Bright Star	50,000⁰K	Blue-White
Be	B0	Orion	25,000⁰K	Blue
A	A0	Sirius	11,000⁰K	Blue-White
Fine	F5	Procyon	7000⁰K	White
Girl	G0	Capella	6000⁰K	Yellow
Kiss	K0	Arcturus	4500⁰K	Orange
Me."	M5	Betelgeuse	3000⁰K	Red

p. 34—(1) Mercury <u>88 days</u>, (2) Venus <u>225 days,</u> (3) Earth <u>365 days,</u> (4) Mars <u>2 years,</u> (5) Jupiter <u>22 years,</u> (6) Saturn <u>29 years,</u> (7) Uranus <u>84 years,</u> (8) Neptune <u>165 years,</u> (9) Pluto <u>248 years.</u> Note: Pluto is usually the planet farthest from the sun. Neptune currently is the planet farthest from the sun. This will change in 1999 as Pluto will then be the farthest planet from the sun. 1. Earth, 2. Mercury, 3. Venus, 4. Mars, 5. Jupiter, 6. Saturn, 7. Uranus, 8. Neptune and Uranus, 9. Pluto, 10. Uranus, 11. Neptune, 12. 5 years, 13. 248, 14. 4

p. 35—Largest to smallest—Jupiter, Saturn, Uranus, Neptune, Earth, Venus, Mars, Mercury, Pluto

p. 36—Pleiades, Pisces, January 1, Capricornus, Sagittarius, Scorpius, Corvus, May 1

p. 40—1, 2, 3, 3, 4, 5, 6, 7, 8. Answer to riddle: Because she was struck by a 9 lb. (4 kg) meteorite that came through the roof of her home.

GA1084

p. 44—Chart A: Spring, Summer, Fall, Winter—Chart B: Prevernal, Vernal, Aestival, Serotinal, Autumnal, Hibernal (Hiemal). **March 21, September 21, June 21, December 21**

p. 46—Right to left on playground and numbers shown below phases, 1, 2, 3, 4, 5, 6, 7, 8

p. 48—A: Sun, B: Heelstone, C: Lentil, D: Trilithon. Length of shadow: 1″ or 2.5 cm

p. 50—1. Cassiopeia, 2. Cepheus, 3. Draco, 4. Big Dipper, 5. Little Dipper

p. 52—1. Day 1, 2. Day 2, 3. Day 3, 4. Day 7, 5. Costa Rica, 6. 9 days

p. 53—1. Right Aileron, 2. Cowling, 3. Right Wing, 4. Spinner, 5. Propeller, 6. Nose Gear, 7. Engine, 8. Landing Gear, 9. Left Wing, 10. Left Aileron, 11. Landing Flap, 12. Fuselage, 13. Horizontal Stabilizer, 14. Elevator, 15. Vertical Stabilizer, 16. Rudder, 1. Climb, 2. Dive

p. 54—1. tail rotor, 2. tail boom, 3. landing gear, 4. engine, 5. controls, 6. cockpit, 7. main rotor, 8. rotor hub, 9. mast, 10. drive shaft. Clockwise

p. 55—Flashback: Igor Sikorsky

p. 56—Parts: (left, up, right, down) 1. engine, 2. engine holder, 3. flameproof wadding, 4. folded parachute, 5. nose cone, 6. shock cord, 7. body tube, 8. launch lug, 9. fins, 10. igniter. Rocket cycle: 1. lift-off, 2. thrusting flight, 3. burnout, 4. coasting flight, 5. apogee (highest point), 6. ejection of recovery system, 7. parachute release, 8. recovery descent, 9. touchdown. Flashback: Robert Goddard

p. 58—A = Doldrums, B = Trade Winds, C = Horse Latitudes, D = Prevailing Westerlies, E = Polar Easterlies, Earth turns West to East

p. 60—0 = < 1 m/hr (< 1 km/hr) , calm, (O); 1 = 3m/hr (1-5 k/hr) light air ( ); 2 = 4-7 m/hr (6-11 km/hr) light breeze, ( ); 3 = 8-12 m/hr (12-19 km/hr) gentle breeze ( ); 4 = 13-18 m/hr (20-28 km/hr) moderate breeze ( ); 5 = 19-24 m/hr (29-38 km/hr) fresh breeze ( ); 6 = 25-31 m/hr (39-49 km/hr) strong breeze ( ); 7 = 32-38 m/hr (50-61 km/hr) moderate gale ( ); 8 = 39-46 m/hr (62-74 km/hr) fresh gale ( ); 9 = 47-54 m/hr (75-88 km/hr) strong gale ( ); 10 = 55-63 m/hr (89-102 km/hr) whole gale ( ); 11 = 64-73 m/hr (103-117 km/hr) storm ( ); 12 = 12-17 = 74 + m/hr (117 + km/hr) hurricane ( ); (not shown on page)

p. 63—Igneous: 1. granite, 2. basalt, 3. obsidian, 4. diorite

Metamorphic: 1. slate, 2. schist, 3. marble, 4. quartzite

Sedimentary: 1. conglomerate, 2. sandstone, 3. limestone, 4. shale

p. 64—Possible order: cards 1-6 in order

p. 66—(W) Evaporation, (E) Condensation, (T) Precipitation

p. 68— 0 △ □ ▭ · ⊙ + − × ÷ Y ··

p. 69—1-4. varies, 5. George Washington Carver, 6. 732-6887

p. 72—Molt

p. 74—Milkweed

p. 75—A = swallowtail adult; B = monarch adult; C = swallowtail caterpillar; D = monarch caterpillar

p. 76—1. B, 2. M, 3. M, 4. B, 5. B, 6. M, 7. M, 8. B, moth

p. 77—1. beige and brown, 2. egg-shaped and colored, 3. bright green, 4. front four are red, then yellow with blue along the sides, 5. black and fuzzy, 6. winter or early spring, 7. will vary, 8. egg, caterpillar, cocoon, adult

p. 78—Raft

p. 79—Walter Reed, Washington, D.C.

p. 80—.⊙. .

p. 82—Ladybird

p. 84—Leap

p. 86—A = roots, B = trunk, C = seed, D = branch, E = twig

p. 87—3 = D, 4 = A, 5= B, 6 = C, 7 = D

p. 88—Pome

p. 89—Shape of a star. Johnny Appleseed. Apples have five seeds. Occasionally, however, an apple may have less. If less, the resultant offspring may be deformed or grow crooked.

p. 90—DNAR

p. 92—Flow: F matched with xx, L ♀ O xy, W ♂

p. 94—P Day 1, R Day 7, E Day 13, G Day 23, N_1 Week 5, A Week 9, N_2 Week 14, C Week 26, Y Week 38

p. 96—Age

p. 102—1. B, 2. R, 3. A, 4. I, 5. N

p. 104—GROWING$_2$ O$_2$LDER$_2$

p. 110— +, −, ∿, ⌢

p. 111—1. AC, 2. DC, 3. AC, 4. AC, 5. AC, 6. AC, 7. AC, 8. DC, 9. AC

p. 112—Will light: A, C, D, E, F, H, I   Won't light: G, J, K, L

p. 114—1. Open, 2. Complete, 3. Static, 4. Open, 5. Series, 6. Parallel, 7. Fluorescent, 8. Dry, 9. Insulator, 10. Series, 11. Nonmagnetic, 12. Generator

p. 115—1. Closed, 2. Short, 3. Static, 4. Closed, 5. Parallel, 6. Series, 7. Incandescent, 8. Wet, 9. Conductor, 10. Parallel, 11. Magnetic, 12. Motor

p. 116—20552 kWh. Thomas Edison

p. 120—A = red, yellow, green; B = red; C = green; D = yellow; E = red

p. 122—Galileo Galilei

p. 123—Period of pendulum is determined by length of string, not weight of bob

p. 124—4, 5, 10, 1, 13, 19, 14, 17, 20, 9, 3, 6, 8, 2, 12, 7, 15, 16, 18, 11

p. 126—Sequence: 1. Piston moves down cyclinder, 2. Intake valve opens, 3. Fuel-air mixture drawn into cylinder, 4. Piston moves up cylinder first time and squeezes fuel-air mixture, 5. Spark plug ignites mixture, 6. Burned gases push piston down, 7. Piston moves up cylinder the second time, 8. Exhaust valve opens, 9. Burned gases pushed out by piston

p. 127—A = lawn mower, 2 stroke   B = automobile, 4 stroke

p. 128—Flush

p. 129—About 60-75 seconds. Five to seven gallons (20-28 liters) used

p. 130—A = Rinse, B = Wash, C = Spin

GA1084

Part Five
Glossary and Index of
Key Science Cycle Concepts

1. Adolescence (96) — The process of growing to maturity. The period of life from childhood or puberty to maturity. This occurs in males in 14th-25th years, females from 12th-21st years.

2. Adult (72) — A person who has passed the age of adolescence and reached maturity; also a full grown plant or animal.

3. Adulthood (97) — State of having reached full growth and maturity.

4. Agitator (130) — One who stirs up, excites, disturbs. A machine mechanism that stirs or shakes.

5. Aileron (53) — A small, hinged plane wing surface, operated by the pilot of an airplane as a stabilizer.

6. Alternating Current (110) — To take turns. In electricity it is current that reverses its direction at fixed intervals of time.

7. Amphibian (84) — An animal or plant able to live on land and in water; an airplane that can take off and land either on land or on water.

8. Amps (Amperes) (119) — The unit of measuring the force of an electric current.

9. Analemma (42) — A graduated scale in the shape of a figure eight indicating the sun's declination and equation of time for every day of the year. Found on globes and sundials.

10. Anatomy (85) — The science of the bodily structure of animals and plants. Also the skeleton or human body.

11. Anemometer (61) — Instrument for measuring speed and pressure of wind.

12. Apogee (56) — The point at which any body going around the earth or another star is farthest away from it.

13. ARC (122) — Segment or part of a circle. The luminous glow which results from the passing of an electric current between two incandescent electrodes.

14. Armature (118) — (1) Armor, a protective covering for defense (2) A piece of iron which connects the two poles of a magnet to stabilize magnetic power (3) Rotating portion of a dynamo.

15. Atmosphere (58) — (1) The air enveloping the earth (2) The kind of air prevailing in any place.

16. Atom (108) — A particle of matter, the smallest unit of an element.

17. Autumnal (44) — Pertaining to autumn, fall, the period between summer and winter; from autumnal equinox to winter solstice.

18. Axis (59) — The straight line, real or imaginary, passing through a body and upon which it revolves or is imagined to revolve.

19. Ball (128) — A spherical or almost spherical body.

20. Beaufort Scale (60) — A scale on which successive ranges of wind speeds are assigned code numbers 0 to 12 or from 0 to 17, corresponding to names from calm to hurricane.

21. Behavior (73) — The actions or reactions of persons or things under specified circumstances.

22. Big Bang (27) — The cosmic explosion that marked the origin of the universe according to the Big Bang Theory.

23. Big Dipper (51) — A cluster of seven stars in the constellation Ursa Major, four forming the bowl and three the handle of a dipper shape.

24. Blossom (88) — A flower or mass of flowers of a plant that yields edible fruit.

25. Bob (123) — (1) A hanging or swinging weight as on the end of a pendulum (2) To nod (3) To cause to move jerkily (4) To clock the tail of a horse (5) To cut short.

26. Buds (88) — Little swellings on the stem of a plant or on the branch of a tree which open into leaves or flowers.

27. Caterpillar (75) — The wormlike larva of a butterfly or moth.

GA1084

28.	Cell (90)	The smallest structural unit of an organism capable of independent functioning.
29.	Chainwheel (125)	Wheel around which the drive chain of a bicycle fits or runs.
30.	Circadian (103)	Exhibiting approximately 24-hour periods; used to describe rhythms that are exhibited by many organisms.
31.	Circuit (112)	A path or route which, if followed without reversal, returns you to the starting point.
32.	Circumpolar (33)	A star that, from a given observer's latitude, does not go below the horizon.
33.	Clockwise (55)	In the same direction as the rotating hands of a clock.
34.	Cold-blooded (84)	Having a body temperature that varies with the external environment.
35.	Coma (37)	(1) A deep prolonged unconsciousness usually the result of injury, disease or poison (2) Nebulous luminescent cloud containing the nucleus and major portion of the head of a comet.
36.	Comet (36)	A luminous body moving through the heavens and following an orbit about the sun.
37.	Compost (64)	Decayed plant material used for helping the growth of plants.
38.	Conception (94)	The formation of a zygote capable of survival and maturation in normal conditions; the beginning of life in an ovum.
39.	Condensation (66)	The physical process by which a liquid is removed from a vapor or vapor mixture or the liquid so removed.
40.	Constellation (45)	A group of fixed stars to which a group name has been given.
41.	Control Panel (131)	A panel upon which various instruments and measuring devices are displayed which are used to control mechanical devices.
42.	Core (31)	The heart or innermost part of anything.
43.	Coriolis (59)	A fictitious force used mathematically to describe motion relative to a uniformly rotating frame of reference such as the earth.
44.	Cosmologists (26)	Those who study the nature of the world as an organized whole.
45.	CO_2 Carbon Dioxide (98)	A colorless, odorless, incombustible gas formed during respiration, combustion, and organic decomposition.
46.	Counterclockwise (55)	Opposite to the left-to-right movement of clock hands.
47.	Crescent (46)	The figure of the moon as in its first quarter, with concave and convex edges terminating in points.
48.	Current (113)	(1) The flow of anything in a stream as a current of a river, a current of air, an electrical current (2) The amount of electrical charge flowing past a point per unit time.
49.	Cylinder (126)	The chamber in which a piston of a reciprocating engine moves.
50.	Daylight (43)	The light of day; the period from dawn to dusk; revolution.
51.	Decomposers (64)	Plants, animals and small microscopic creatures living in the soil which break down plants and animals.
52.	Diaphragm (99)	A thin stretch of muscle that separates chest from abdomen. Used in breathing.
53.	Direct Current (110)	A current that flows in only one direction in electricity.
54.	Diurnal (76)	Daily, happening every day; opposite of nocturnal.
55.	Disk (35)	A thin, flat circular plate.
56.	Dormant (86)	Sleeping or inactive, latent but capable of being activated.
57.	Drag (52)	Something that retards motion, the retarding force exerted on a moving body. Drag is the component of air reaction which is parallel to the air stream.
58.	Egg (72)	One of the female reproduction cells of various animals, usually consisting of an embryo surrounded by nutrient material with a protective covering.
59.	Electricity (114)	Physical phenomena arising from the existence and interaction of electric charge. An imponderable and invisible force of nature, used by man to produce light, heat and power.

60.	Electroencephalography (102)	The study of the electrical activity of the brain.
61.	Electrons (108)	A minute particle of matter charged with the smallest known quantity of negative electricity; opposite of proton.
62.	Enzyme (64)	A substance that promotes a chemical change but does not change in itself.
63.	Equator (42)	The imaginary circle dividing the earth into two equal parts, the north and south hemispheres.
64.	Equinox (44)	A point at which the sun goes across the equator.
65.	Evaporation (66)	To pass off in vapor or give off vapor. The act of water changing from a liquid to a gas.
66.	Exhale (99)	The giving out of breath or gas.
67.	Flap (53)	(1) A flat usually thin piece attached at only one side (2) Variable control surface on the trailing edge of an aircraft wing used to increase lift or drag.
68.	Flush (129)	To be cleaned by a rapid brief gush of water.
69.	Frequency (111)	The number of cycles per second produced by the generator of an alternating electrical current.
70.	Galaxy (28)	Any of numerous large-scale aggregates of stars, gas and dust, containing an average of 100 billion solar masses (Milky Way).
71.	Gears (125)	Toothed wheels or cylinders that mesh with other toothed elements. To transmit motor or to change speed or direction.
72.	Gibbous (47)	The moon more than half, but less than fully, illuminated.
73.	Gnomon (48)	An object, as the style of a sundial, that projects a shadow used as an indicator.
74.	Goober (69)	Regional word for peanut.
75.	Gravity (52)	(1) The force that tends to draw all bodies toward the center of the earth. (2) A result of the natural attraction between massive bodies.
76.	Habitat (81)	The region in which an animal or plant naturally lives or the place where a thing is usually found.
77.	Heart (100)	The organ in animals by which blood is pumped through the system.
78.	Heelstone (48)	A solitary vertical stone at Stonehenge, which is one of the stones, used about 1900 BC to 1400 BC as a religious center and an observatory from which predictions of astronomical events could be made. (Conjectured as a sighting post.)
79.	Hertz (111)	A unit of frequency equal to one cycle per second.
80.	Horizontal (57)	Related to the horizon level, not vertical.
81.	Horoscope (39)	A representation of the heavens at any given time by which astrologers profess to foretell the future of persons born at that time.
82.	Igneous (62)	(1) Pertaining to fire (2) Caused by action of fire and heat inside the earth, fused, as igneous rocks.
83.	Inhale (99)	The taking in of breath or gas.
84.	Insecticides (79)	One who, or that which, kills insects.
85.	Intersections (121)	The places where two things meet or cross.
86.	Kilowatt (116)	One thousand watts, which are defined as a unit of power equal to one ampere of current pushed by one volt of electromotive forces.
87.	kWh (Kilowatt Hour) (117)	A unit of electric power consumption indicating the total energy developed by a power of one kilowatt acting for one hour.
88.	Larva (72)	The wingless often wormlike form of a newly hatched insect before undergoing metamorphosis. The early stage in the changes of other animals that pass through several phases of development.
89.	Latitude (42)	The angular distance north or south of the equator, measured in degrees along a meridian as on a map or globe.

90.	Legume (69)	(1) A two-valved seed vessel having a row of seeds attached along the seam where the parts join (2) A plant bearing legumes.
91.	Lentil (48)	(1) A plant of the pea family with edible seeds (2) A horizontal slab of stone connecting two trilithons.
92.	Life Cycle (104)	The series of stages through which an individual organism passes in its progression through life.
93.	Lift (52)	Power or force available for raising.
94.	Light-year (29)	The distance that light covers traveling in a vacuum for a period of one year. Approximately 9.46 trillion kilometers or 5.878 trillion (5.878×10^{12}) miles.
95.	Lungs (100)	Spongy, saclike respiratory organs in most vertebrates, functioning to remove carbon dioxide from the blood and provide it with oxygen.
96.	Magma (62)	The molten matter under the earth's crust, from which igneous rock is formed by cooling.
97.	Matter (27)	That which occupies space and is perceptible by the senses.
98.	Meat (68)	The flesh of animals used as food.
99.	Menstruation (93)	The process or an instance of discharging the menses (blood and dead cell debris that is discharged from the uterus through the vagina by adult women at monthly intervals).
100.	Metamorphic (62)	Relating to metamorphosism which is an alteration in composition, texture or structure of rock masses caused by heat or pressure.
101.	Metamorphosis (74)	Change in structure or habits of an animal during normal growth. In insects the emerging of an adult from a maggot. In amphibians, emerging of frog from tadpoles.
102.	Meteoroid (40)	Any of numerous celestial bodies ranging in size from specks of dust to asteroids weighing thousands of tons, which appear as meteors when entering the earth's atmosphere.
103.	Meteorite (40)	A stony or metallic mass which has fallen upon the earth out of space; surviving from meteors.
104.	Milky Way (28)	The galaxy in which the solar system is located, visible as a luminous band in the night sky.
105.	Mohs' Scale (63)	A measure of hardness or resistance of a substance to scratching, or to indentation under a blow or steady load. Ten minerals are used as reference points from talc (hardness 1) to diamond (10).
106.	Molts (80)	Shedding an outer covering such as feathers, cuticle or skin which is replaced periodically by a new growth.
107.	Neutrons (108)	A particle of matter without electrical charge. It and the proton combine to form nearly the entire mass of atomic nuclei.
108.	Nocturnal (76)	Pertaining to night. Active at night.
109.	Nucleus (37, 109)	The central mass around which matter accumulates or grows. A complex protoplasmic body within the living cell that contains the cell's hereditary material and controls its metabolism, growth, and reproduction.
110.	Nutrients (64)	Something which nourishes. A nourishing ingredient in a food.
111.	Nymph (80)	One of the young of any insect that undergoes incomplete metamorphosis.
112.	OBAFGKM (32)	System of spectral classification of stars embodied in the Henry Draper catalogue embracing classes OBAFGKM (ranging from the hottest to the coolest stars). The spectral sequence represents a group of stars of essentially the same chemical composition but of differing temperature and atmospheric pressures.
113.	Observe (115)	To make a systematic or scientific observation or watch intently.
114.	Orbit (34)	The path of a celestial body or man-made satellite as it revolves around another body and one complete revolution of such body.

115.	Organ (90)	A differentiated part of an organism adapted for a specific function.
116.	Organ Donation (106)	The willing or giving of an organ of a deceased person to another for use in an organ transplant.
117.	Organisms (65)	Living individuals; plants or animals.
118.	O₂ Oxygen (98)	A free element, a gas without color or smell, occurring in the lower atmosphere of the earth in abundance; essential to all life, animal or vegetable.
119.	Ovary (89)	The seat in a female organism of the eggs or carpels that beget new life.
120.	Pedals (125)	Treadles or foot levers, as on a bicycle or organ.
121.	Pendulum Period (122)	The time from any point on the swing of a pendulum to that point again.
122.	Perennials (86)	A plant living for three or more years, normally flowering and producing fruit the second year and every year thereafter.
123.	Period (92, 122)	(1) An instance or occurrence of menstruation (2) The time interval between two successive occurrences of a recurrent event.
124.	Phase (46)	A distinct stage of development. One of the cyclically recurring apparent forms of the moon or a planet.
125.	Pitch (54)	A steep downward slant and the degree of such a slant.
126.	Planet (34)	A nonluminous celestial body illuminated by light from a star, such as the sun around which it revolves.
127.	Plants (68)	Any vegetable organism(s).
128.	Pods (69)	The covering of certain seeds as of the pea and bean, holding the seeds in a row.
129.	Pointer Stars (50)	Two stars in Ursa Major, the line of which points to the North Star.
130.	Polaris (33, 50)	A star of the second magnitude at the end of the handle of the Little Dipper and almost at the north celestial pole.
131.	Pollinated (89)	To convey or transfer pollen from the anther to the stigma of a plant or flower in the process of fertilization.
132.	Pome (89)	A fleshy fruit having seeds but no stone, such as the apple, pear, or quince.
133.	Power (56, 118)	The rate at which work is done, work with respect to time expressed in watts or horsepower. The product of applied potential difference and current in a direct current circuit.
134.	Precipitation (66)	Water droplets or ice particles condensed from atmospheric water vapor and sufficiently massive to fall to the earth's surface, such as rain or snow.
135.	Predator (82)	An animal that lives by preying upon others.
136.	Pregnant (95)	About to have offspring; carrying a developing fetus within the uterus.
137.	Prey (83)	(1) A creature hunted or caught for food (2) To hunt, catch, or eat as prey.
138.	Protons (108)	The smallest units of positive electricity.
139.	Puberty (92)	The stage of maturation in which an individual is capable of sexual reproduction.
140.	Pulse (101)	The rhythmical throbbing of arteries produced by regular contractions of the heart.
141.	Pupa (72)	The inactive stage in metamorphosis of many insects, following the larval stage and preceding the adult form.
142.	Radiant (41)	(1) Emitting heat or light (2) The apparent celestial origin of a meteor shower.
143.	Rectifier (111)	A device, as a diode, that converts alternating current to direct current.
144.	Recycling (70)	Extracting and reviving useful substances found in waste.
145.	Red Giant (30)	Any of certain stars of great size giving out a feeble red light.
146.	Respiration (99)	The complex physical and chemical processes by which plants and animals take in oxygen (O₂) and give off carbon dioxide (CO₂).
147.	Revolutions (124)	The motion of a body around a point outside itself as that of the moon around the earth.

GA1084

148.	Rings (87)	Circular object form, or arrangement, with a vacant circular center. An annual ring around a tree.
149.	Rootstock (88)	Or rootstalk—a shoot that grows entirely underground sending roots below and shoots with foliage above; a source.
150.	Rotation (59)	The act of turning on an axis or hub; the act of alternating, first one and then another, as rotation of crops.
151.	Rotor (55)	A revolving or rotating part in machinery. Assembly of rotating horizontal air foils, such as that of a helicopter.
152.	Rudder (53)	A vertical hinged plate mounted at the stern of a vessel for directing its course. The same thing at the tail of an aircraft for the same purpose.
153.	Sapling (87)	(1) A young tree (2) A youth.
154.	Sedimentary (62)	Of or pertaining to rocks formed from sediment or from transported fragments deposited in water.
155.	Seedling (87)	A young plant which is grown from seed.
156.	Shell (109)	Any set of hypothetical spherical surfaces centered on the nucleus of an atom that contains the orbits of electrons having the same principal quantum number.
157.	Sleep (102)	A natural periodical recurring physiological state of rest, characterized by relative physical nervous inactivity, unconsciousness, and lessened response to external stimuli.
158.	Soil (65)	Land, earth, that part of the surface of the earth that can be dug, plowed, and planted; any substance in which something grows.
159.	Solid Waste (132)	Waste in a solid, as opposed to liquid or gaseous form, which is resistant to change in form.
160.	Solstice (44)	One of the two points in the sun's seeming journey through the sky; winter, summer.
161.	Spiral (28)	A curve winding away from a center, as if going upward around the surface of a cone.
162.	Sprocket (125)	A wheel with teeth on the outer rim to engage the links of a chain; one of the teeth or cogs on such a wheel.
163.	Stages (105)	Levels, degrees, or periods of time in the course of a process. A period or phase in the development of anything.
164.	Star Trails (33)	A continuous line produced on a photographic plate by the image of a star during an exposure in which the camera or telescope does not follow the diurnal motion of the star or follows the motion of some other celestial body (as a comet) that is being photographed.
165.	Steam (67)	The vapor phase of water.
166.	Stopper (128)	A device, as a cork or plug, inserted to close an opening.
167.	Stroke (127)	Any of a series of movements of a piston from one end of the limit of its motion to the other.
168.	Sunrise (49)	The event or time of the daily first appearance of the sun above the eastern horizon.
169.	Sunset (49)	The event or time of the daily disappearance of the sun below the western horizon.
170.	Sunspot (31)	Any of the relatively dark spots that appear in groups on the surface of the sun that have an approximate 11-year cycle and are associated with strong magnetic fields.
171.	Supernova (30)	A rare celestial phenomenon involving the explosion of most of the material in a star, resulting in an extremely bright, short-lived object that emits vast amounts of energy.
172.	Swarm (79)	A large number of insects or other small organisms, especially when in motion.
173.	System (90)	A group of interacting, interrelated, or independent elements forming a complex whole.
174.	Tail (37)	The rear end of anything. Anything hanging loose.

175.	Temperatures (45)	The degrees of hotness or coldness of a body or environment as indicated on or referred to a standard scale.
176.	Thrust (52)	The forward-directed force developed in a jet or rocket engine as a reaction to the rearward ejection of fuel gases at high velocities.
177.	Time (51)	Measure of duration, as by hours, days, years, ages.
178.	Tissue (90)	The substance fiber, or texture, of which an animal or plant body is formed.
179.	Traffic (120)	Movement of vehicles on street or highway.
180.	Transformer (111)	An induction coil to raise or lower the strength of an electric current.
181.	Trilithon (48)	An ancient stone monument consisting of two upright megaliths carrying a third as a lintel.
182.	Tropic of Cancer (42)	Small circle of the celestial sphere parallel to the celestial equator 23 1/2° north of the equator. Limit of sun's northern latitude.
183.	Tropic of Capricorn (42)	Small circle of the celestial sphere parallel to the celestial equator 23 1/2° south of the equator. Limit of the sun's southern latitude.
184.	Tubercles (77)	Small rounded prominence or process, such as a wartlike appearance on the roots of some leguminous plants or a knoblike process in the skin or bone.
185.	Tumbler (78)	(1) One that tumbles (gymnast) (2) Drinking glass.
186.	Universe (26)	All existing things including the earth, the heavens, the galaxies and all therein, regarded as a whole.
187.	Uterus (92)	A pear-shaped muscular organ of gestation that is located in the pelvic cavity of female mammals and receives and holds the fertilized ovum during the development of the fetus and is the principal agent in its expulsion at birth.
188.	Valve Seat (129)	A seat into which the valve moves in order to stop or regulate the flow of a liquid or gas.
189.	Vernal (44)	Of, or pertaining to spring, springlike.
190.	Vertical (57)	At right angles with the horizon, pointing straight up.
191.	Volts (119)	The international system unit of electrical potential and electromotive force equal to the difference of electrical potential between two points on a conducting unit carrying a constant current of one ampere where the power dissipated between the points is one watt.
192.	Water Cycle (66)	Hydrologic cycle—the circulation of waters of the earth between land, oceans, and atmosphere. Evaporated from oceans, precipitated to land as rain, returned to the atmosphere by transpiration (plants) and rivers and streams back to the ocean.
193.	Water Vapor (67)	Water diffused as a vapor in the atmosphere, especially at a temperature below the boiling point.
194.	White Dwarf (30)	A faint, very dense star that has a radius approximately that of the earth.
195.	Wriggler (78)	(1) The larva of a mosquito (2) One that wriggles.
196.	Yolk (91)	The nutritive material of an ovum consisting primarily of protein and fat, especially, the yellow, spherelike mass of the egg of a bird or reptile.
197.	Zodiac (38)	(1) An imaginary strip in the sky on each side of the sun's path, including 12 major constellations and used by astrologers in predicting the future (2) A band of the celestial sphere 8° to either side of the ecliptic that represents the path of principle planets, moon, and sun.

GA1084

Meet the Author

Jerry is a teacher at The University of Toledo. He is a member of the Department of Elementary and Early Childhood Education, and his specialty is science, although he truly enjoys all facets of education and life.

Jerry was born and raised on a farm in Kaukauna, Wisconsin, and it was there that he nurtured his interest in science, the world around him and life in general. He has taught all grade levels in some capacity or another and currently spends a great deal of his time in schools helping teachers and youngsters.

In addition to being the author of 19 books (available in such prestigious places as the Smithsonian Institution in Washington, D.C.: National Air and Space Museum, National Museum of Natural History—National Museum of Man, National Museum of American History) and over 150 educational publications, Jerry is the recipient of many awards. Some of these include the 1984 Outstanding Teacher of the Year Award at The Univeristy of Toledo, the 1986 Martha Holden Jennings Outstanding Educator Award, and the National Science Teachers Association 1986 Search for Excellence in Science Education Program Award.

Being a local, state, regional, national and international consultant in science education, Jerry's main interest in life is to help people grow in awareness, knowledge, and understanding of feelings toward themselves and others. His works nurture this interest.

Peaceful Cycling,

Jerry De Bruin

And Artist

Elaine is the mother of three and has worked with children in and out of the home for the past twenty years. She received a B.F.A. degree and teaching certificate from Bowling Green State University and is presently a preschool teacher at Fairgreen Nursery School in Toledo, Ohio. She pursues her interests in art and science by bringing the concept of "hands-on" science into her preschool classroom, nurturing a love and appreciation for science in young children.

Happy Cycling,

Elaine Scott

GA1084